Happiness W...

George E. Vandeman

about the author

No one who has heard George Vandeman speak, or has read his books, will deny that there is a simplicity and charm, as well as a forcefulness of conviction, that is refreshing. Here is an empathy with his readers, a rapport that penetrates to the need of the individual. The books talk. They do not read.

In each of the author's books—and their circulation is now into the seventh million—the kindness and conviction of the personality that holds an audience comes through on paper. The words cease to be ink marks and become the throbbing reflection of all that the reader has ever felt—and only wished he could say.

George Vandeman's background includes pastoral ministry, direct evangelism, the training of ministers, and speaking to huge audiences on both sides of the globe. His outstanding contribution to the faith of this generation, however, is through the IT IS WRITTEN telecast. It is difficult to escape the thought that God has especially prepared him for this ministry to the multitudes.

And now you hold this book in your hand. It is not by accident. Rather, it may be by divine appointment that you read its pages. But you will never regret the moments you spend. And don't be surprised if you are never quite the same again!

by
GEORGE E.
VANDEMAN

Happiness
WALL TO WALL

PACIFIC PRESS
PUBLISHING ASSOCIATION

Mountain View, California
Oshawa, Ontario

TO MY WIFE NELLIE,

whose love, companionship, and down-to-earth wisdom have made our home a delightful demonstration of
HAPPINESS WALL TO WALL

Copyright © 1968 by
Pacific Press Publishing Association
Litho in U.S.A. All Rights Reserved

Fifteenth Reprinting, 1984

Library of Congress Catalog Card No. 68-56328

ISBN 0-8163-0054-2

Contents

1. Happiness Wall to Wall   1
2. Formula for Two   13
3. Marriage Isn't Easy   27
4. Trouble With the Personnel   38
5. Teen-age Dilemma   50
6. Bribing the Gatekeeper   67
7. When the Rain Falls   79

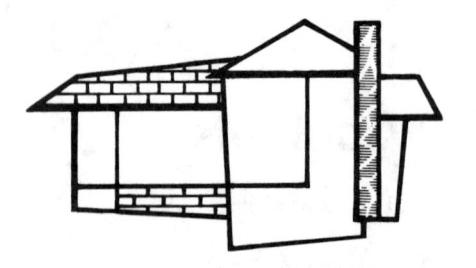

1.
Happiness Wall to Wall

WHAT do you do when the raft comes apart?

It's an exciting moment when one man and one woman are launched together into the swift-moving waters of matrimony —with happiness just downstream. But what do you do if, out in the rapids, the raft comes apart? Do you attempt to tie the pieces together? Do you look for a branch that might hang out over the current, close enough to grasp? Do you call for help?

Bill, in San Diego, looks up from his noonday sandwich and startles his friend with the question, "Say, you have a happy home. What's your secret?"

Sandy, in Detroit, speaks softly into the telephone. "I know, Mom. I never thought it could happen to us."

Bob, in Wichita, steps into a quiet waiting room. A few minutes later in the private office, he says, "I never thought I'd ever see a marriage counselor. But maybe you know some secret that I don't. God knows I've tried."

Carol, in New York, sits across from her pastor in his study. "I don't know what has gone wrong. We both expected happiness. But it has been a straight road into a living hell."

Kent, in Chicago, looks his father straight in the eye. "Dad, do you think there is any way of picking up the pieces now—

after all this? I guess we read the road signs wrong, or something. Our marriage just didn't take."

The raft has come apart. And disillusioned husbands and wives from Maine to California are trying to tie the pieces together. They are looking for some sturdy branch which they can grasp in a final attempt to hold the raft steady. They are calling for help, each in his own way, but with the same common desperation.

And then, one spring morning, a little irritated by the clear blue sky and the singing of the birds, Bill in San Diego, Sandy in Detroit, Bob in Wichita, Carol in New York, and Kent in Chicago, step into elevators grim and determined and beaten, push the button for their floor, and step into the office of their attorney. They are filing for divorce.

They don't want divorce. They don't believe in divorce. They have tried to postpone this day. But home has become something even worse than an open marital breakup.

Each of them is about to become another statistic. These five abandoned marriages will be included in 450,000 divorces granted this year. As statistics, ten disillusioned marriage partners will join the fifteen million other Americans who are divorced. Their children? They will join the ranks of four million boys and girls who, as the aftermath of divorce, must face the future with half, or less than half, the parents they deserve.

But Bill and Sandy and Bob and Carol and Kent are more than statistics. They are human beings. The one nagging thought in their minds is that they have failed in life's greatest adventure. Their pride and their self-confidence are undermined.

Sandy and Carol find themselves disorganized, moody, un-

Happiness Wall to Wall

able to concentrate, worried about the children but with no one to share their concern. They are bitter, overwhelmed, and lonely.

Bill and Bob and Kent are haunted by the fact that their own children don't really belong to them anymore—and never will.

The children cry themselves to sleep at night because they still love both parents—and feel guilty because this is so.

Yet Bill and Sandy and Bob and Carol and Kent, with their mates, five or ten or fifteen years ago, stood in happy anticipation before the altar—like countless couples from many generations—and repeated after the minister, "Till death do us part." They clasped hands as they heard the words, "What therefore God hath joined together, let not man put asunder."

Never were promises more eagerly made. Their every dream included the word "forever." What has happened? Why have their promises become only statistics? What is the secret of lasting marriage? What is it that keeps untainted, unmarred, unshattered, the inexpressible joy of the wedding day?

Is marriage nothing more than candlelight and romance that soon burns out? How does it work in a five-room house with four walls, three children, a restricted budget, and a custom-made problem or two? Can there still be happiness—wall to wall?

The truth is that locked within the marriage contract lie either the potent seeds of devastating emotional difficulties, or the strong foundations for enduring success. Which will it be? Will marriage be a ceremony—or a creation? Will it be a duel—or a duet? Will the raft carry you safely to happiness? Or will it come apart?

Reminds one, doesn't it, of the winsome prayer of the Brittany fishermen, "Keep us, O God! The sea is so big, and our boats are so little!"

Is marriage always what the partners expect it to be? Does it obediently follow their blueprint?

A lovely young wife, after four years of marriage, was discussing needed marital adjustments with her pastor. Charming in her feminine chatter, she turned back into the fairyland of her courtship dreams. She had been wedded in a beautiful church service to a fine young man. She looked forward to never-ending enchantment, travel, affection without end, clothes fit for a princess, and barrels of money. Yes, and endless energy to enjoy all these things—like a bubbling artesian well.

Now she seemed to say, "Why didn't you tell me that there would be a shift of scenery?" She sensed now that she would have to accept the realities of homemaking. She needed to adjust to babies, dishes, bills, and hard work without compromise.

No marriage is a feature-length romance of ecstasy. Even the best marriages are the product of pull and stress, strain and concern. Successful relationships are forged in the crucibles of daily tasks and daily challenges.

Yet what man would be courageous enough when he proposed marriage to ask, "Would you be willing to work eighty hours a week for me for nothing? Would you cart home from the market and prepare something like 500,000 pounds of food? Would you wash a mountain of dirty dishes as large as a sizable ski jump—just for love? Will you wash and iron the clothes on a line forty-seven miles long with two extra miles of specialty items added for each baby? Will you climb to the top of the Washington Monument for me 12,000 times—just for love?"

Happiness Wall to Wall

No. Marriage is not an endless honeymoon. It is an endless sharing of the tasks and responsibilities of making a home. The newness will wear off. The glamour of courtship will not always continue. But does the fabric of spontaneous companionship have to wear as thin as it does?

In early marriage the husband extends his hand and helps his wife alight from the car as if she were a Cinderella on her way to a ball. But now, if she delays a moment, he walks ahead and calls back, "Come on, honey. We don't have all day!"

Does it have to be that way?

In courtship days he often admires the softness of her hands. He is captivated by her date-fresh hairdo. True, her hands, in time, may show a little dishpan red. Her hairdo may suffer an occasional tussle with the wind. But does the husband, looking forward to a little beauty and romance, have to come home from work only to have her meet him at the door with curlers in her hair, in a frayed housecoat, slippers that don't match, and a lifeless, unscrubbed complexion? Is it really surprising that he blurts out, "What have you been doing all day?" and goes seeking better scenery?

Is such a letdown inevitable? Do marriages really have to deteriorate from the very beginning? Must reality always bring disillusionment?

One young couple had dated under the usual social conditions. But they decided to test their love in a different setting. Every night for a week he came to her home, where they cooked dinner and washed the dishes together. Then they sat in the living room and talked. No radio. No TV. No record player. They simply talked together all evening. He then said good night and walked out. They wanted to be certain, before spending a lifetime together, that they could stand each other under such realistic conditions without being bored.

You see, happiness is not a state of continuous laughter, perpetual excitement and hilarity. It is not found in continual flitting from one fun spot to another. Happiness is the preparing of a meal. Happiness is watching little children grow from infancy to adulthood. It is cooking and freezing, spading the garden, washing the car, walking in the woods, shopping for the family, eating homemade bread, watching a blazing sunset.

Marriages do not have to come apart in midstream. But they will if you are not agreed on your destination. They will if the knots are not securely tied. They will if you underestimate the pull of the current. They will if you come to the rapids unprepared.

Marriage is life's greatest adventure. But it is also the most frightening voyage you can take.

You see, when you marry, you do far more than take to yourself a wife, or a husband, and the obligations of marriage. You take into your hands, as a sacred trust, a bit of human destiny. The man or woman you marry is more than a body to be clothed and fed. There is a soul as well. When you face the Judge of all the earth, a time that is repeatedly and reverently described in Scripture, you stand absolutely alone before your God. But here is a matter in which you face eternal responsibility for all given to you by marriage or by birth.

It becomes mighty important, doesn't it? Worth working at. Worth building it right, beginning it right. Worth a solid foundation.

Said the psalmist, "Except the Lord build the house, they labor in vain that build it." Psalm 127:1.

How important are the foundations of a marriage? Burgess and Cottrell, pioneer researchers in the field, discovered that vows said in a religious marriage service, with the approval of both sets of parents, were most lasting. Those married by a justice of the peace were more unhappy than happy. When the husband stopped going to church before he was eleven years of age, the couple was one tenth as happy as the average. If husband and wife continued attending church until they were nineteen and attended two thirds of the time after marriage, they were 50 percent happier than the average couple.

This is just a statistical way of saying what Martin Luther discovered. After his marriage to the nun across the way, he spoke of the miracle of Jesus at the wedding feast when He turned the water into wine. Luther commented that if Jesus is not in your marriage, life is tasteless and without zest. But when Jesus comes into your home He always changes the water into wine. His presence transforms the ordinary and common routine into experiences of zest and sparkle. He takes away the drudgery. He takes away the coldness of duty and puts everyday happiness in its place.

Evidently it is possible to build a marriage so satisfying that heaven will seem to us neither far away nor strange—because our own hearthside has known the touch of heaven here and now.

But the possibilities against such a success in marriage are tremendous. There are so many places to get off course, so many potential areas of misunderstanding, so many situations that will not yield to common sense alone, so many circumstances the marriage manual does not fit, that the wonder is that any marriage ever succeeds. If it does succeed, not alone on the surface but in its unseen everyday relationships, it is because a sincere willingness to learn is combined with the miracle of the presence of Him who created both marriage and its personnel.

Marriage, I say, is a frightening adventure. It is a linking of destinies that we would scarcely risk were it not for the pull of the heart. Imagine! Two people who have never lived together, who know little about each other, suddenly undertake to live together the rest of their lives, from this day forward!

Good fortune, sorrow, failure and disgrace, sickness and health—all will be shared. And more than that, by their commitment they lay themselves open to a whole new range of dialogue and hurts and problems never before possible.

The more sensitive they are to happiness, the deeper will be the wounds. The higher the expectations, the keener will be the disappointments. The more unselfish the devotion, the more crushing the betrayal.

What do you bring to your marriage? Are you asking what your mate can do for you—or what you can do for your mate? It makes all the difference. For if the marriage relation is nothing more than pooled selfishness, it hasn't a chance.

There will be conflict in marriage. It cannot be otherwise. For the personal intimacy that is inherent in all the everyday relationships of marriage is inseparable from a degree of conflict. Intimacy creates a certain amount of tension. In a strange paradox it creates the wounds it heals. Why? Because in marriage each partner exposes himself to the most critical scrutiny of the other. And that other has probably entered into marriage with exaggerated expectations. Reality is honest. But it is also frightening. Two distinct personalities here attempt to fuse as one. And marriage is only the beginning. To be fully known, and yet be fully loved—that is the goal.

Happiness Wall to Wall

Marriage, you see, makes each partner peculiarly vulnerable to the other. For it exposes every weakness, every difference of opinion. It exposes every failure of one to meet the expectations of the other. It opens up limitless possibilities for hurt.

How quickly can happy anticipation turn to disappointment! I am reminded of the young husband who was counseled by his minister to remember that he had taken his bride for better or for worse. "Yes," he replied, "but she is worse than I took her for!"

When two people have joined hands in matrimony, there is no longer any room for pretense. They must abandon all masks and poses, all games. The continuous intimacy of married life will expose them all for what they are. Simplicity and sincerity are vital. Yet how rare are those virtues today! Happy is the man or woman who brings them to his marriage.

Dwight Hervey Small has said it so well: "Modern society trains us to be subtle and sophisticated, indirect and devious, clever. We live by exaggeration and affectation. We become experts at impression, masters at pretense. . . . We express emotions we do not feel. . . . We prefer the world of make-believe."–*Design for Christian Marriage,* page 59.

There is no place for pretense and parade in marriage. No place for window dressing. Only authenticity will pass the test. But you can bring to your marriage that priceless gift of genuine sincerity if you will. Success in marriage is not easy. But thank God it is possible!

Remember Bill—and Sandy—and Bob—and Carol—and Kent?

Could it be that portraits of these five problem homes could spotlight your need or mine? Are they a composite picture of marriage in distress? And if you find yourself identifying with one of them, is it not because human nature, wherever it is found, displays a likeness to itself?

Bill, in San Diego, doesn't really know what is wrong with his marriage when he asks his lunchtime friend for advice. He only knows that communication in his home is hopelessly blocked. He really blames his wife. But he is a husband who won't talk. His father was a man of few words. And he is the same. Why should his wife need reassurance of his love? He works his head off for her, doesn't he?

And now, she won't talk either. If both partners had realized that the communication system is the heart of a marriage, if some simple principles had been understood and practiced, could not this rift have been avoided? It makes one think of the words of Hosea 4:6: "My people are destroyed for lack of knowledge."

Sandy, in Detroit, would tell you a different story. She was an only child, brought up in a rather strict home. She felt her freedom restricted and seized upon an early marriage as a form of protest. At first she tried to live up to most of the principles she had been taught. Her husband admired her for it, and it looked as if their marriage might succeed. Then he began bringing home some of those stimulating, bluntly suggestive magazines and paperbacks from the newsstand. She wouldn't read them. She hid them. Then she read just one. And that was the beginning.

It was not long before the moral fiber of their marriage began to weaken. Yet, compared to what they were reading, their own activities seemed above reproach. The decay was almost imperceptible at first. But finally there was this other couple—and the wife-swapping episode that ended in divorce. Sandy would tell you it didn't need to happen.

Happiness Wall to Wall 11

Bob, in Wichita, thinks the trouble is in his marriage. He still doesn't realize that the trouble is in himself. He simply has not learned the basic principles that would enable him to get along with people—people anywhere, on the job, in social contacts, in any human relationship. He has moved from one job to another, never really understanding why. His wife was patient really. They separated several times for a few weeks, but always tried it again because of the children. Finally they just stopped trying. A second marriage for Bob won't stand a chance unless he learns that the trouble with marriage is trouble with the personnel.

Carol, in New York, has experienced perhaps the most dramatic tragedy of the five. Actually, she and her husband came from almost identical backgrounds. Both came from small towns. Both had good homes. Both encountered the claims of Christ in their teen-age years. She decided for her Lord. He did not. She was counseled to reconsider the marriage. She was troubled by the words of the apostle: "Be ye not unequally yoked together with unbelievers." 2 Corinthians 6:14. But her case was different. She thought his religious background would hold him steady—even if he didn't live his convictions. Now, however, she describes their marriage as a straight road into a living hell. She can't explain it. She can only reluctantly tell it. At first their paths began to diverge only slightly. Then they moved to the city, and her husband's love for the sensational began to create a problem. He was curious about hypnotism—curious enough to want to probe just a little. Then he began to experiment with drugs—just to see what the magazines were talking about. He urged Carol to join him in his new adventures. That, of course, she could not do. Then finally came that psychedelic weekend. Marital disaster. A straight road into a living hell. And she really should have known.

Kent, in Chicago, is the man who has everything—promising job, suburban home, interesting social life, enviable bank account, a charming wife and three lovely children. That is, he did have a wife and three lovely children—until the divorce. He may find another wife to grace his home and share his social life and his bank account. But his children aren't really his anymore. And they can never be replaced.

He is the man who has everything—except an active faith in God. He is not really an unbeliever. He believes. But he wants to keep his faith boxed in so that it can't touch his work life, his social contacts, or even his home. Why should his kids have religion fed to them with a spoon? When they are old enough to make a choice, they will make a choice. His wife didn't really need to make such an issue of it. But now she has the children. The house is strangely quiet. And what went wrong with his marriage? Why didn't it take? Why wasn't it stable enough to stand a little gust of wind?

Can homes like these be saved? Can the raft be steadied and tied together before the killer rapids are reached? Can the vulnerabilities of marriage be better understood, blocks in communication removed, dangers spotlighted, personalities protected, rifts avoided, minds kept strong, by facing problems honestly?

I think so. That's why you hold these pages in your hands!

2.
Formula for Two

HAPPY marriage is not a glamorous package that the partners discover in the huge pile of wedding gifts. It is not something made and stored in heaven ready to be handed out to any two applicants. Rather, it is a do-it-yourself project. It has been suggested that it is like one of those kits which comes knocked down for putting together. It will take some gluing, some sanding of rough spots. Hammering a bit. Filing down the scratches. Planing, carving, bending, varnishing—and then backing off to take a look. Dusting and waxing and polishing until at last you recognize it as a dream fulfilled.

What is it that makes a house a home? What is it that transforms a collection of people into a happy family? What is it that makes home a father's kingdom where the wife is queen, every daughter a princess, every son an heir—and where Christ reigns over all? Evidently the family tie is the closest, the most tender and sacred on earth. Listen!

> Love is not passion, love is not pride;
> Love is a journeying side by side.
> Not of the breezes, nor of the gale—
> Love is the steady set of the sail.

> Deeper than ecstasy, sweeter than light,
> Born in the sunshine, born in the night,
> Flaming in victory, strongest in loss,
> Love is a sacrament made for a cross.

I think right here you want me to share with you the Scripture formula for true love. It is not only a *formula for two*, but a formula for getting along with people anywhere. For in every relationship in life it's people that make the problem. Listen to 1 Corinthians 13:4-7, reading from the New English Bible:

"Love is patient; love is kind and envies no one. Love is never boastful, nor conceited, nor rude; never selfish, not quick to take offence. Love keeps no score of wrongs; does not gloat over other men's sins, but delights in the truth. There is nothing love cannot face; there is no limit to its faith, its hope, and its endurance."

There you have it! God's *formula for two*. Read it again and again. Evidently we are here dealing with a dimension in human relationships that has been little understood. For here is emphasized so precisely the value of the individual—the other individual. So often it has been overlooked. And as a result the partner's sense of security has been threatened.

I am not talking about a bank account. I am talking about security in the other's affections. For I have discovered that a sense of security and a feeling of personal worth are as important to a man or a woman as life and health. Nothing can so quickly encourage happiness in marriage as to build in your mate a sense of security in your affection, the feeling of being valued and loved and needed. Without such a foundation happiness will have a very short life.

Formula for Two 15

Check yourself by the divine formula—if you dare. I promise you, the revelation may be disturbing. At least, I found it so. Are you patient? Are you kind? Are you boastful and conceited, sometimes rude? Are you selfish and sensitive, quick to take offense? And tell me, do you keep a score of wrongs, slights, and injustices that come your way? Are you quick to watch out for your rights, careful to see that they are recognized by others?

Bruce Barton tells a little-known story from the experience of Abraham Lincoln. In the early months of the Civil War, Lincoln and a member of his cabinet went to call on General McClellan. Official etiquette prescribes that the President shall not call upon a private citizen. But the times were too tense for protocol. Lincoln needed firsthand information and McClellan was the only man in Washington who could give it.

The General was not at home, and the two men waited in his parlor for an hour. Finally they heard him at the door and supposed that he would speak to them immediately. But without a word he hurried upstairs. They waited another thirty minutes. Finally Lincoln asked one of the servants to remind the General that they were still waiting. After a few moments the servant returned and told them, with obvious embarrassment, that McClellan had said he was too tired to see the President. In fact, he had already undressed and gone to bed.

When the two men were outside the house, the cabinet member exploded in anger. Should not Lincoln instantly oust McClellan from command? But the President laid his hand quietly on the other man's shoulder. "Don't take it so hard," he said. "I'll hold McClellan's horse, if he will only bring us victories."

Why was Lincoln willing to accept this insult to his dignity?

There was a great purpose in his heart to win the war and to free a race. That was his passion. His pride, his position, his dignity, his rights took second place.

That's how the formula works. That's how it works in public life. That's how it works in the home. "Love seeketh not her own." The destiny of the home, the future of two souls, the happiness of our mate—these come first. Our own rights, our dignity, the respect due us—these come second. Strangely enough, happiness can more easily find us when we are standing second in line.

I have discovered, too often the hard way, that the secret of lasting marriage is made up of little things—little unselfish acts, little words, little courtesies, little attentions. Why is it that we have kind words for others through the day, but when we cross the threshold of our own homes there is a tendency to let down? Why—when we love our own the best?

> We have careful thoughts for the stranger,
>   Sweet smiles for the sometime guest,
> But oft for our own, the bitter tone,
>   Though we love our own the best.

> —Margaret Sangster.

The threshold of home can be a lift instead of a letdown. We need not leave tact and human kindness on the office desk. You love your family deeply. But do they know it? Do we take too much for granted?

Christianity in the home, you see, includes appreciation and kindness and culture and simple courtesy, as well as uprightness of character. Bluntness, painful frankness, the brand of

Formula for Two

honesty that always says what it thinks, no matter how unkind—these are not virtues, but faults. They do not belong in the home. In fact, they do not belong in any relationship.

The four walls of home were meant to enclose happiness, not to shut it out. Home should be more than a temporary shelter for wounded sensitivities and broken hearts. And it can be. When Christ is in the home, it will be a place where we give our own the best, where the simple attentions and courtesies of courtship come as naturally as the day they were born.

A choice story that my wife Nellie discovered in her reading and which I have told around the world is that of a couple about to celebrate their golden wedding anniversary. (And incidentally, did you know that, even with the eroding elements of this twentieth century, one fifth of our marriages last more than fifty years?) In this instance a local newspaper sent out a reporter for an interview, and the husband was at home.

"What is your recipe for a long, happy marriage?" the reporter asked.

"Well, I'll tell you, young fellow," the old gentleman said slowly. "I was an orphan, and I always had to work pretty hard for my board and keep. I never even looked at a girl until I was grown. Sarah was the first one I ever kept company with. When she maneuvered me into proposing, I was scared stiff. But after the wedding her pa took me aside and handed me a little package. 'Here is all you really need to know,' he said. And this is what was in the package."

He reached for a large gold watch in his pocket, opened it, and handed it to the reporter. There across the face of the watch, where he could see it a dozen times a day, were written these words: *"Say something nice to Sarah."*

Too simple to work, you say? But it did. Just remember

that great happiness is purchased by small, inexpensive tokens. Thoughts of appreciation pay. Criticism does not. Understanding, tender affection, freely expressed—these build a happy relationship.

But sometimes kindness and appreciation are pushed aside and forgotten. Sometimes, I have painfully discovered, there has to be some mending done, some verbal repairing, some changing of heart, some assuming of personal blame. Every marital raft fit to face the gale will have to have the ropes tied a little tighter now and then before risking the rapids.

High on the list of happy marriages that I have known about is that of Bob and Helen. Dr. Charles Shedd recalls the details.

Bob was a pusher, and she was retiring. He was the life of a party; she stayed in the shadows. Yet they seemed perfectly mated. You would see them holding hands and exchanging a sly smile as if they were reading some silent message between them.

One night they gave a dinner party. Several times Bob went to the kitchen and offered to help. Finally she let him pour the water. And then, when all was ready, he served her first! I don't know what book of etiquette he had been reading. But she sat there beaming, as if it was supposed to be that way.

The whole dinner was a thing of beauty. Several times in the conversation he asked her opinion on some subject—and even listened while she expressed it.

After dinner a guest took Bob aside and asked him the secret of his happy marriage.

"I tell you," he said, "it hasn't always been this way. The first couple of years of our marriage were pretty rough, until we were ready to call it quits. Then one day we decided to

Formula for Two

make a list of all the things we didn't like about each other. The lists were pretty long, but Helen gave me hers and I gave her mine. It was pretty rough reading. Some of the things we had never said out loud or shared in any way.

"Then we did what sounds like a foolish thing. We went out to the backyard to the ash can and burned those lists, watched them go up in smoke, while we put our arms around each other for the first time in months. Then we went back into the house, and we each made a list of all the good things we could dig up about each other. This took a little time. It was hard, because we were pretty down on our marriage. But we kept at it.

"Then we did another thing that might look silly to you. Come on back to the bedroom and I'll show you." He led his friend to the neat, attractive bedroom. And there at the focal point on the wall, in two maple frames, were two scratchy lists.

"If we have any secret, it is this," Bob confided. He told how he had memorized his list while driving to work, how he kept repeating it every day. And he said, "Now I think she is the most wonderful person in the world. And I guess she feels the same about me. That's all."

That's all? But it goes to the heart of a great marriage—this canceling out the bad and building up the good. Theirs was homemade heaven! With two scratchy lists on the wall!

Remember what the apostle Paul says? "Love keeps no score of wrongs." Take them out to the ash can—literally. Burn them up!

Friend, your relationship may need some mending. If it does, remember that the strong threads of kindness and appreciation are the most lasting material you can use.

Every home needs mending. Every home has misunderstandings. Every home has disagreements. But the longer I live and the more people I meet, the more I realize that the most delicate care must be used in settling these conflicts. For differences of opinion, in the loaded, dangerous atmosphere of criticism and blame, are highly explosive.

Here is good counsel for your home and mine. Never quarrel at breakfast. Many a husband has torn out of the driveway, spinning gravel on his way to a collision, after a breakfast-table quarrel. And many a wife has spent her day in regret. Now follow through. Never quarrel when he comes home from work. A husband can stand almost anything at work if he has a happy home. Never let him come home to a nagging wife. And then, never quarrel after lights are out. It spoils the day.

In fact, my counsel would be simply, Never quarrel! There are no good quarrels. Let the steam off some other way. Quarrels never clear the air—they only poison it. Quarrels only scar. Current books to the contrary, a fight is a fight, whether the weapons used are fists or adjectives. Word wounds are often worse than those made by clubs.

Have you read "The First Settler's Story" recently? That time-worn tale is one of pathos, but it contains a lot of wise counsel for married hearts. You remember the young settler came home tired after a long day's work. For some reason, without his wife knowing it, the cows had escaped. And he blamed her for it. "You had nothing else to do!" he said. "You could at least have watched the cows!"

Immediately he regretted his bitter words. But the damage was done. He felt led to beg her forgiveness that night, but his pride stood in the way. The next morning he was in a hurry and left reconciliation for another time.

Formula for Two

Late in the afternoon he saw a storm coming up and headed for home. The cabin was empty. But there on the table was a note. "The cows have gone again," it said. "I'm sorry. I tried to keep them in. Please have kind words for me when you come home. I have gone to find the cows."

His wife? Out in that storm? He hurried after her, caring nothing now about the cows. She had not realized the severity of the storm that now broke in all its fury. While lightning tore across the sky, ripping it into deafening crashes of thunder that released a blinding hail, he searched frantically for his dear one. All night he combed the hills and valleys. Then with the morning sun he returned to the cabin, only to find her limp body lying not far from where he had killed her with his tongue. It was too late—*too late for words!*

> If I had known in the morning
> How wearily all the day
>   The words unkind
>   Would trouble my mind
> I said when you went away,
> I had been more careful, darling,
>   Nor given you needless pain;
> But we vex our own
> With look and tone
>   We might never take back again.
>
> For though in the quiet evening
> You may give me the kiss of peace,
>   Yet it might be
>   That never for me
> The pain of the heart should cease.

> How many go forth in the morning
> > That never come home at night,
> And hearts have broken
> For harsh words spoken
> > That sorrow can ne'er set right. . . .
>
> "Oh, lips with the curve impatient,
> > And brow with that look of scorn,
> 'Twere a cruel fate
> Were the night too late
> > To undo the work of the morn."
>
> —Margaret Sangster.

In any home, I say, there will be differences of opinion that need to be discussed. It is a good rule never to go to sleep at night until misunderstandings have been cleared up, if there have been any. The apostle Paul says, "Never go to bed angry—don't give the devil that sort of foothold." Ephesians 4:26, 27, Phillips.

I believe you will regret any deviation from this plan. Differences are best approached in the quiet, uncharged atmosphere of tenderness and understanding, with forgiveness freely granted. For misunderstandings, if not cleared up promptly, become set in the mind as attitudes, and can eventually ruin a marriage.

And now I want to ask you a question. You love your wife. You love your husband. But have you ever thought of him, or her, as your best friend? Stop just here for a moment and think it through. Your best friend. Basically, husband and wife are friends. Wouldn't this idea relax many a strained relationship?

Formula for Two

Friends. Don't friends do things together? Don't friends share things together? Are you letting your marriage become only an assumed responsibility, rather than a spontaneous friendship? Someone has said that love is friendship set to music. Is it that way with you? Or are you trying to keep the love when the friendship has long been lost? Are you drinking from the brazen cups of duty while you could be drinking from the golden chalices of friendship?

Do things together. And it doesn't stop with husband and wife. Every child that enters the home needs attention. He needs *two* dedicated parents. He needs their time. He needs the sacrifice of selfish plans. Happy families play together, work together, explore life together, build a boat together— even if it leaks. Just ask my boys and my daughter Connie about the boat that leaked. Go camping together. It doesn't matter so much what you do. But do it together. Memory tells me I should have done it more.

And another secret. When couples, and families, learn to pray together, they will have discovered an important factor in preventing marital difficulties. Family prayer was once an established institution. When it declined, up went home problems and divorce. The number of people who go on week after week, month after month, year after year, without family devotions, is simply appalling—many of them professed Christians.

What about prayer in *your* home? God said through Jeremiah, "My people have forgotten Me days without number." Jeremiah 2:32. Makes one think, doesn't it?

In one home where a Christian mother had passed away, the little girl told a stranger in awed and frightened tones, "We haven't had prayer in our house since Mother died, and *nothing has happened yet!*"

What a poor, limited conception of what prayer really means! Are our children being taught that prayer is merely a fire escape? No, nothing had happened in that home. Nothing but slow, imperceptible decay.

God isn't going to strike us dead. He loves us too much for that. There probably won't be any serious calamity aside from spiritual disintegration. And thus gradually we lose out just when we think we are strongest.

Worship in the home, making the home Christ-centered, can be a most happy experience in the lives of our children. They need not be made to feel that prayer time is an unwelcome duty or a burden.

A word just here. The devotional program of one home may not be best for another. The schedule of family devotions will need to be tailored to the needs of your home. This is what I mean. The ideal, it would seem, would be to gather the family together for prayers both morning and evening. But suppose that you have tried it. It worked fine in the morning. But when you attempted it after the evening meal, the children complained, the phone rang constantly, and everybody had to wait. Tableclearing, dishes, and homework were all delayed. Everybody went to bed tense and cross. But you had had your family devotions!

That, for your home, may not be the best plan. Then you might try continuing with the family group together for morning worship. But at bedtime let each parent spend time individually with each child—talking over any problems, praying together. Let each child look forward to this time with Father and with Mother that is completely his own. In my own home we followed the first plan as our two older boys were growing up. Now, with the younger son and my daughter, we find the

Formula for Two

second plan happier. There is a right way, a best way, ... home. Find it—and then follow it consistently.

No amount of family devotion, of course, can take the place of your own time alone with God. But even here there is a right way—a way that will help, not prejudice, the lives that you touch. In one home the father rose early each morning for meditation and prayer alone in his den. His small daughter followed him one morning, but was told to "get out of here." She asked her mother what daddy was doing. And mother said, "He's trying to learn to love the people downtown."

Love the people downtown? And lose one's own? Fortunately that father saw his mistake, and soon it was not unusual for one of the children to join him in his morning prayer.

Is it possible to overestimate the saving influence of a Christian home? Children may wander in the wilderness for a while during the disturbing upheaval of adolescence. But the memory of consistent, honest dedication in the home will never be erased. God said through Isaiah, "I will contend with him that contendeth with thee, and I will save thy children." Isaiah 49:25.

I read somewhere of a young father who had wandered away from God. He had reached the end of his rope. He thought of suicide. Then God touched his life, and he began a new relationship with his family.

He had a boy who was not doing well in school. He had begun to steal things around the neighborhood to gain attention. He was lonely and rebellious. After only two weeks the boy said to his father, "Dad, what's happened to you lately?" The father said slowly, reaching for the right words, "Well, Son, I guess I was making a pretty big mess of my life, and I decided I'd ask God to take over and show me how to live it."

The boy looked down at the floor. "Dad," he said quietly, "I think I'd like to do that too."

The father stood there with tears running down his cheeks, and he and the boy wept together. The next day the father left for New York on a business trip lasting two weeks.

He was anxious to get home. When his plane taxied up to the terminal, his son broke through the crowd and ran out to meet his father. His eyes were bright with excitement. "Dad," he said breathlessly, his voice full of wonder, "do you know what God has done?"

"No, Son. What has He done?"

"He's changed every kid in my class!"

Friend, God can change every heart in your home. And He can do it now!

3.
Marriage Isn't Easy

IN THE early days of the South a rather strange ceremony was contrived by plantation owners for slaves who desired to be married. The couple would be asked to join hands and jump over a broomstick three times. Then the plantation owner would say, "I pronounce you man and wife until death or distance do you part."

Eyebrows lift today at the thought of being married by jumping a broomstick. But I ask you, What might history say of a generation who *dissolved* marriages by rapping a gavel? Are we doing any better? Is divorce the solution? Is it an easy back door out of an unpleasant situation?

It is a sacred moment when two people who were strangers to each other are drawn together by an irresistible attraction so that they cannot from that moment be divided by time or space.

When a man sees in one woman that dream of purity and sweetness that has ever haunted his soul, or when in one man a woman finds the love and satisfaction that she has been unconsciously seeking, they can know that they have found the basis for lasting happiness.

It was to protect and prolong that sacred moment that those memorable words were spoken by Him who was the

Creator, "What therefore God hath joined together, let not man put asunder." Matthew 19: 6.

Countless radiant couples from many generations have echoed these words as they have repeated after the minister, "Till death do us part."

Now there are promises to keep. Will it be easy to keep them in a world where morality is treated as nothing more than an academic issue to be tossed to the experts? Will it be easy to keep them in a society whose moral fabric is tearing at the seams? Will it be easy to keep them in the days when happiness has become an uneasy peace that intermittently retreats behind the truce lines? Will it be easy to keep them in a materialistic circle that confuses happiness with possessions?

No. In a world like this, marriage isn't easy!

Unfortunately, this delightful arrangement given by God has in too many cases been so cheapened and abused that it has little resemblance to what God intended it to be. Holy wedlock has too often been transformed into unholy deadlock.

Many marriage partners—and their number is legion—are caught in a desperate struggle to save their marriage. Some are frankly confused, not knowing why or how their hopes have been so bitterly blasted. Others are distressingly aware that some personal failure is responsible for their difficulty.

As a result, divorce has assumed fantastic proportions. Someone has said, "Let's call marriage a belt that we can buckle and unbuckle." In other words, if you don't like it, just unhook!

Marriage has become a cloak, blessed and sanctioned by society, to be sure, but to be cast off at will. One young socialite flitted from one mate to another so often that a

Marriage Isn't Easy

society columnist suggested the need for a wash-and-wear wedding gown. And one young man boasted before his wedding, "If it doesn't work I will have saved enough on my income tax to get a divorce next year."

God never intended that sacred relationship to be either assumed or discharged so lightly. Yet Dr. Karl Menninger, the famous Kansas psychiatrist, predicts that shortly every family in North America will be touched by divorce somewhere.

Aldous Huxley, in *Brave New World,* carries it to a shocking extreme. He says that if the recent rate of divorce continues to accelerate, "In a few years, no doubt, marriage licenses will be sold like dog licenses, good for a period of twelve months, with no law against changing dogs or keeping more than one animal at a time."

It may be all right for a spaniel, friend. But not for men and women made in the image of God.

Loose marriages, easy divorces, and broken homes are constantly yielding a harvest of bitter tears and broken hearts. Or worse still—festering wounds, deep-seated resentments, bitterness, and hatred that are actually poisoning the springs of life and inviting disease and even death.

Is there an answer to the world's marital dilemma? To whom may one turn?

Some seek the answers of popular psychology, and some have been helped. But psychology without Christ has its limitations. I have walked the floor through the night with men who were in desperate personal struggle—some of the keenest scientific minds, men themselves trained in the art of giving the best counsel. They knew all the answers. Yet these answers, short of the power of God, we discovered, were totally inadequate for their own needs. The only ladder that could bring these men out of tangled, bitter confusion was the insight, the commitment, the surrender that made the cross of Christ its center and its power.

Christ in the home. This is the ideal. But in spite of the recent surge of religious interest, we are reaping the harvest of a generation of moral abandon, a generation of release from restraint and taboo. For a taboo, we were told, stunted the personality. And so the Ten Commandments were tossed aside as out of date. They just didn't fit into our so-called progressive thinking. Our morals stretched like rubber bands.

Then openly published Kinsey reports and the like convinced us that we were not so bad after all. And psychologists, psychiatrists, and ministers have been overworked ever since.

Is it any wonder that marriages today burn briefly like a paper chain and then are gone?

"Till death do us part." The secret of happiness in marriage is not difficult or profound. Turn back the pages; listen again to the charge on that youthful wedding day as the minister repeated:

"I charge you both that if you wish your new estate to be touched with perennial beauty, cherish those gracious visions which have made springtime within your hearts during the days of your courtship. You must never forget nor deny the vision you once saw; you must resolve that it be not blotted out nor blurred by the commonplace experiences of life. Faults may appear which were once hidden in a golden mist; excellencies may seem to fade in the glare of the noonday sun. Still be unmoved in your devotion; still remain confident and hopeful. Amid the reality of present imperfections believe in the ideal. You saw it once, and it still exists."

What has happened? In a shocking number of cases the

Marriage Isn't Easy

ideal is forgotten, and divorce stands at the doorstep. Somewhere along the line the sacred confidence of the family circle has been broken. That moral reserve and dignity that cause the careless and the loose to keep their place have been lost. Advances have been made, hearts broken.

And you don't have to look very far for the root of the trouble. For down in the heart of those discarded Ten Commandments is a very reasonable warning which, if obeyed through the power of God, would guard the purity of the race: "Thou shalt not commit adultery."

However relaxed the moral fabric of the society in which we live, however benumbing the repeated assertion that everybody does it, however convincing the published reports of moral decadence with which we subconsciously compare ourselves, still, God says, "Thou shalt not commit adultery."

Whatever professional advice may have been given you to the contrary, the Creator of man's body, his mind and emotions, the God who understands our fears and our frustrations and our needs—it is He who says, "Thou shalt not commit adultery."

God calls it adultery. Many, today, call it a meaningful relationship. Any behavior is said to be all right if you call it love. And you decide what to call it while in the grip of an emotional situation.

Only occasionally does a lone voice like that of David Redding come through. He says, "Proponents of the new morality claim that the commandments may be broken in order to fulfill the higher law of love. True, the Christian idea is to do the unique will of God for each special situation. But God never needs to sacrifice principles to satisfy any situation. If we try to keep the commandments even when they appear most inappropriate, God always comes through. . . . The laws stand and perhaps are most in force when we feel least sure. What are any laws good for except for those very occasions when we are being most tempted to abandon them? This God who thinks of everything . . . tailors His laws beautifully to every situation. And if we can hang on to the commandments at the fiery moment when we are certain that keeping them will ruin us, God will do His amazing part, just as He did for Daniel standing that night in the lions' den."–*The New Immorality,* pages 58, 59.

Are the restrictions of God's moral code unreasonable? Is there no better way to rediscover the thrill of living than to fall into some stupid adultery?

There's the problem. How can a man expect marriage to succeed if he has destroyed the barrier that the Creator Himself has placed around it? Can he carelessly ignore the first indiscretion, and not expect a flood of infidelity to come in?

Listen. The break-up of a marriage doesn't happen all at once. It begins with the first neglect of the little attentions that make happiness for a companion. It begins the day you are too tired to be kind, too busy to be thoughtful, too occupied with your own problems to be interested in those of your mate.

Infidelity doesn't happen all at once. The act of adultery is a blow from which the home may never recover. But much has gone before. Infidelity begins when first the relationships of home become routine and dull. Infidelity begins when a man begins to shift his interests from an evening at home to an evening at the shop. Infidelity begins when the husband begins to compare his wife's beauty with that of another, or when she

Marriage Isn't Easy 33

begins to compare her husband's success with that of another. Infidelity begins when he or she first questions the wisdom of their marriage.

Infidelity begins in an unguarded moment. It ends in a betrayal that can forever shatter the confidence of the one you promised to love and cherish.

In answering a question of the Pharisees, our Lord made His position on the matter of divorce and remarriage very clear. Let me read His words from Dr. Phillips's translation of Matthew 19:3-9:

"Then the Pharisees arrived with a test question. 'Is it right,' they asked, 'for a man to divorce his wife on any grounds whatever?'

" 'Haven't you read,' He answered, 'that the One who created them from the beginning made them male and female and said: *"For this cause shall a man leave his father and mother, and shall cleave to his wife; and the twain shall become one flesh"?* So they are no longer two separate people but one. No man therefore must separate what God has joined together.'

" 'Then why,' they retorted, 'did Moses command us to give a written divorce notice and dismiss the woman?'

" 'It was because you knew so little of the meaning of love that Moses allowed you to divorce your wives! But that was not the original principle. I tell you that anyone who divorces his wife on any grounds except her unfaithfulness and marries some other woman commits adultery.' "

Have you noticed the ease with which some rationalize around the difficulty in order to exchange mates? Yet from what we have read it is clear that the trivial excuses some use to become separated from their companions could scarcely stand the test of Scripture. Jesus gives us the one situation in which a man or a woman is free to remarry. It is simply this—when he or she discovers himself to be the innocent party in a moral fall.

Love, of course, will do all within its power to forgive and restore. It will not grasp at the sin of a mate as a welcome opening for release. For a divorce, however legitimate, not only seriously mars your own life but tragically undermines the lives of your children.

How often a couple will say, "We think our marriage may go on the rocks. But after all, that is definitely *our* business."

No, friend. Marriage is everybody's business. Each divorce, it is estimated, touches forty or fifty lives. It is a nation's business. Every time a home is destroyed, the whole nation suffers a tremor. It is the child's business. The child, like a seismograph, registers every marital quake. It is God's business, because He wanted to use your love, father and mother, to explain His own love to a child. And now He can't!

"Pastor Vandeman," someone says, "I was divorced and remarried a number of years ago. I didn't consider it seriously then. Most all of our friends were doing it. I'm not sure who was the more innocent or the more guilty, for I didn't care. What shall I do about it now?"

The Word of God has an answer for that sincere inquiry. However serious your marital mixup, please know that if you are deeply and sincerely repentant, you have a God who forgives. "Though your sins be as scarlet, they shall be as white as snow; though they be red like crimson, they shall be as wool." Isaiah 1:18. And this in 1 John 1:9: "If we confess our sins, He is faithful and just to forgive us our sins, and to cleanse us from all unrighteousness."

The Lord has a wonderful way of dealing with matters like

Marriage Isn't Easy

this. But though He forgives, though He never condemns, He always adds, "Go, and sin no more."

But however wonderful this provision, I think you can see how God must feel about the man who searches the rules of the church, any church, to discover how he might have his own way and yet continue in good standing. Friend, if this is your reasoning, please be doubly sure that you are testing your own motives as well as the rules of the church.

May I speak for a moment about the innocent one in a situation involving a moral fall? Is it not possible for an individual to be so selfish, so unattentive, so unloving, so downright cold in his or her relationship to his mate that these unfeeling actions make temptation tragically real and all but force the unconsecrated heart to sin?

Oh yes, as far as the church is concerned, he or she may be the innocent party. But there was one who wasn't willing to love, one who wasn't willing to lay selfishness aside, to win and hold that mate by true affection. Does not that individual share in the guilt?

Friend, is it possible that an attitude of Pharisaic criticism, even though unexpressed, may be destructive to the very one you most want to help? Listen to the words of Dr. Paul Tournier.

"Every judgment that I make of a man, even if I am careful to say nothing to him, even if I hide it deep in my heart, and even if I am almost or entirely unaware of it myself, makes between him and me an unbridgeable gulf and hopelessly prevents my giving him any effective assistance. By my judgment, I drive him more deeply into his faults rather than free him from them."–*Guilt and Grace,* page 80.

These are the words of a distinguished physician and counselor. They apply not only to marriage but to every human relationship. Dr. Tournier continues: "Thus the most tragic consequence of our criticism of a man is to block his way to humiliation and grace, precisely to drive him into the mechanisms of self-justification and into his faults instead of freeing him from them. For him, our voice drowns the voice of God. We put him beyond the reach of the divine voice which can only be heard in the silence. The impassioned response which our criticism triggers off in his soul makes too much noise."

Have you ever been guilty? I have.

Criticism is destructive anywhere. And when it touches marriage, I think you can see how easy it is to drive that first wedge of hidden blame that eventually separates two hearts. Remember, the ruin of a marriage is not always a dramatic affair. There need be no unfaithfulness, no blows, no desertion. It may be just a slow accumulation of dissatisfactions, a gradual growth of misunderstandings and irritations and petty criticisms until one or the other asks himself, "Did I marry the wrong person?"—and feels wicked for thinking it! At last comes the day when one says, "I can't stand it any longer!" And the other is stunned!

No man or woman can be too careful in guarding the sacred circle of marriage. For once it is broken, it is difficult to repair.

But however frustrated and confused a life partnership may have become, however futile may seem your efforts at reconciliation of hearts that have grown cold, please remember that divorce should never be thought of as simply a convenient back door out of an unpleasant situation. Divorce cannot heal. No legal or material device, however ingenious, can heal. Only unselfish love and the power of the living Christ can heal. And

Marriage Isn't Easy

forgiveness—forgiveness strong enough to say, "I leave the past behind and with hands outstretched to whatever lies ahead I go straight for the goal." Philippians 3:13, 14, Phillips.

A husband prayed long and earnestly after he learned of his wife's unfaithfulness. He recounted again the betrayal that threatened his home. But over against it were the words of the apostle, "Be as ready to forgive others as God for Christ's sake has forgiven you." Ephesians 4:32, Phillips.

Finally his prayer was answered. He went to his personal safe and took out a sheaf of letters. Here was costly evidence against her loyalty—evidence that might have set him free. He had kept them against the day when he might use them in court. But now God had forgiven his own sin, and he was willing to cast hers into the fire. As the evidence went up in smoke, he saw disappearing all means of getting even. He saw consumed in flame the whip that he had held over his mate's head. Here had been a weapon to destroy. But in one quick moment the condemning words had been transformed into ashes. He was free now—free to forgive!

4.
Trouble With the Personnel

A YOUNG man asked a physician for the hand of his daughter in marriage. The doctor refused. It was quite a setback, but the young suitor gathered courage to ask, "Why can I not marry your daughter? I love her."

The doctor replied, "I think you do."

"I can support her."

"I suppose you can."

"Then why can't I marry her?"

To this the doctor answered, "My daughter has a miserable disposition. Nobody could live with her and be happy."

The young man gallantly replied, "But there is always the grace of God."

The doctor smiled understandingly. "When you are as old as I am, young man, you will realize that the grace of God can live with some people that you can't live with!"

The trouble with marriage is not with the institution. It's with the personnel. The trouble is with people. It's people that need to be changed. Unhappy couples don't dislike marriage. They dislike each other. The challenge in marriage is not only in *finding* the right person, but *being* the right person. Many a wife has thought she needed a new husband, only to realize that her husband needed a new wife.

Trouble With the Personnel

Too many marriages have gone on the rocks because one partner entered the contract secretly planning to change the other. And it doesn't usually work that way. If a bus says "Cincinnati," that is likely where it is going. You can't count on its changing destinations after you board it. It's the same with husbands and wives.

Glenn Clark, popular author and publisher, has listed some beatitudes of a happy marriage. One of them is this: "Blessed are the married ones who strive first of all to make their mates *happy* rather than *good.*"

The trouble is that so many of us feel it is our duty to make our mates good—and we sometimes make everyone concerned unhappy in the process. I have been guilty. But I have discovered that if we persevere in trying to make our mates happy, we more easily succeed in the other objective.

We are talking here about sound principles of interpersonal relationship. To be sure, they are especially applicable in the unique relationships of marriage where a home must survive or perish. But the same foundation principles will succeed in the relations of friend with friend, doctor with patient, employer with employee. And surprisingly enough, we often discover that the difficulty is not *between* two people, but *within* two people, *within* the individual. Changing your own heart, you see, is likely to be the surest and fastest way to change the heart of your mate.

Why do we continue to struggle with the simplest lessons in personal relations when we ought to be taking an advanced course? One couple visited a marriage counselor after nineteen years of marriage. The counselor told them, "You have not had nineteen years of experience in marriage. You have simply lived the first year nineteen times."

The secrets of marital success are not elusive. I feel strongly that if we would put the hard work and ingenuity into our homes that we put into our jobs, we would succeed.

Tact and insight. These are invaluable in the office environment. They are equally indispensable at home. Human nature does not respond charitably to bluntness. Tact, you see, is saying the right thing, the right kind of thing, at the right time, in the right way. Tact involves not only words, but the tone of voice, the mood, the atmosphere, the motive. And insight is the willingness to understand another's point of view—with the possibility that it may be right. Together they are the healing therapy that reaches into a wounded heart and avoids a crisis. Without tact and insight, marriage too often becomes a savage contest in which each partner tries to wound more deeply than the other.

Why should we be so blind to the fact that we have faults too? The most ideal person has faults. And marriage in itself does not eliminate them. But we get in a hurry. We expect marriage to solve automatically and instantly all the problems we had before marriage.

A college girl knows that it takes time to adjust to a new roommate. A violinist knows that he will not be a professional when first he picks up the instrument. But we expect marriage to be different. We may be unhappy single. We may be miserable in school. We may be in conflict with our parents. But we expect marriage to change us miraculously and instantaneously into ecstatically happy persons. And it doesn't work that way.

It is when we begin to accept life as it is, and our mates as they are, that we begin to move toward a happy home.

A young wife, married about three years, breezed into her pastor's office, tossed her coat over a chair, and exploded,

Trouble With the Personnel

"Honestly, Bill is the most ornery, stubborn, independent, obstinate—ooooh! But you know what? I'm learning to live with him! Now how do you like that?" And then she added, "He's adorable! I would never have believed it possible that I could be so extremely exasperated with a man yet love him so dearly." And she was gone.

Of course, if you are normal, you have probably experienced some degree of marital tension. There are those who say they have never quarreled. That may be true. Or it may be that they are simply giving their quarrels another label. One husband said, "We've never had an argument in thirty years of married life. However, we have engaged in serious discussions which the neighbors heard a block away."

Every home, I say, has some problems. Some homes more than others. A marriage counselor asked one young couple, "What do you have in common?"

The wife replied, "One thing. Neither of us can stand the other."

John Milton, the unhappily married poet, once heard his wife referred to as a rose. He remarked, "I am no judge of flowers. But it may be true, for I feel the thorns daily." And John Wesley's wife used to sit in City Road Chapel and make faces at him while he preached!

Let me repeat again, there are no good quarrels. It is unfortunate that those who write the marriage manuals often think it necessary to include a chapter on how to quarrel. Don't we agree that quarrels only weaken the relationship, each encounter leaving it less secure?

There was the man who said, "Oh, she would never leave me."

"Don't be too sure," said the minister to whom the wife had already come in great distress.

And the man said, "Why, she can't do that to me. What would I do without her?"

The minister asked quietly, "Did you ever tell her that?"

"No," the man admitted. "I don't like such talk."

When it was suggested that he take home some flowers and recourt the woman of his choice, this huge, clumsy-looking fellow exclaimed, "Now wouldn't I look fine luggin' home flowers? I'd feel like a fool." Just the same, he did it. And it broke the growing coolness, stimulated the basic strong original affection between them.

Too simple to work, you say? Don't you believe it. Flowers may not always be the answer. But a lack of appreciation in small things can grow until it becomes a great divisive factor.

Do you take your mate for granted? Or are you attempting, by little acts of thoughtfulness, coupled with the appropriate words, to protect your marriage against deterioration? Is your companion secure in your affection? Does she know, does he know, that no attack from without can shake the ship of matrimony? Do the children know it?

One expert has said, "The most important thing a father can do for his children is to love their mother." How quickly little children are unsettled by dissension in the home! Only when they know that nothing can crack the rock of their domestic tranquillity will they be content.

Do you remember—even in moments of crisis—that your wife is a person—your children are persons? Do you remember their need for a sense of security and a feeling of personal worth? Have you made a determined effort to understand those needs? For tragedy sets in, homes begin to disintegrate, when we do not understand. It starts with little neglects, little misunderstandings, little selfish attitudes— until finally there is

Trouble With the Personnel

constant bulldozing and belittling until the last spark of identity is killed and the heart is drained of its desire to continue!

Nagging, that demonic tactical maneuver in a psychological battle, is often the culprit. Said the wise man, "A continual dripping on a rainy day and a contentious woman are alike." Proverbs 27:15, RSV.

And one modern authority says, "Most cases of emotionally induced illness are the result of a monotonous drip, drip of . . . unpleasant emotions, the everyday run of anxieties, fears, discouragements and longings."—Dr. John Schindler, *How to Live 365 Days a Year*, page 13.

Who can take the drip-of-the-faucet treatment for long—especially when it comes from someone you love?

How can the rift be healed? How can the gulf be bridged? Communication. That is the answer. Talking it over is a cornerstone in building a successful marriage. There should be a willingness to talk at all times. Many a misunderstanding could be healed in minutes if both partners would calmly evaluate it. There is nothing in all of marriage more destructive than the presence of a silent rift.

One wife said, "You know how you feel when the phone rings and nobody answers? That is how I feel."

There is a lifetime of communication ahead of each of us. Wouldn't it be wise to learn the art better? The heart of marriage is its communication system. Communication breakdown is a chief source of trouble in all human relationships—especially in the intimate and continuing relationship of marriage.

It is impossible not to communicate. If we do not communicate with words, we will be communicating by our silence. And our silence may be as easily misunderstood as our words.

The communication in marriage is not the same as communication of courtship. The excitement of exploring each other's lives begins to disappear. The girl who was once so glamorous is now washing dishes. The ability to communicate now, in changing circumstances, may determine whether the marriage survives or not.

Honesty at this point is all-important. Playing games will not do. Wearing masks will not do. Masks cannot communicate. Only people can communicate. And the intimate ties of marriage are never strengthened by pretense.

Those who communicate, in any area of life, face one baffling problem: *Is anyone listening?* Do you hear what your wife says? Or is your mind taking a meaningful excursion elsewhere? It is estimated that we spend about 70 percent of our waking hours in communication of some kind—speaking, listening, reading, or writing. Evidently listening is mighty important.

Marriage, unfortunately, provides no guarantee that the partners will listen to each other, or try to understand each other. Too often when one is speaking, the other is really not present. He is running errands in his mind. The happy lesson to be learned is that love listens. It is only as love listens that love can understand. Listening will do what words cannot. Did you ever try to find the right words to let someone know his opinions are important to you? Listening will do it as if by magic.

Robert Soudek wrote of John F. Kennedy, "He made you think he had nothing else to do except ask you questions and listen—with extraordinary concentration—to your answers."

Sometimes, in the marital relationship, you get a busy signal. If a husband has been barraged with messages all day, he may, without ever knowing it, tune out his wife just as he

Trouble With the Personnel

would a television set. One wife said, "My husband can have the TV and the radio on at the same time, listening to two different games at once. The kids can pester him endlessly with interruptions, yet he can tell you the progress of either game whenever you ask. This is the same guy who can sit at the supper table without any distractions whatever and not hear a word I say."

Evidently we *choose* to listen.

Human nature is so persistent. Speaking, you see, is a way of asserting one's self. Listening is not. That's why it is easier to speak than to listen. This inward need for self-assertion is manifested in many ways. For instance, there is the chronic interrupter who constantly attempts to take the ball. There is the one who breaks into the conversation with "that reminds me" and diverts the topic of discussion into his own channel. Then there is the one who breaks in with "I know just what you are going to say," and thereby robs the speaker of any opportunity whatever for unique expression. Such a listener listens with only one thought in mind—"Where do I come in?"

Then there is the man who is always right. There can be no productive conversation with him. His mind is already closed. Lucy, of *Peanuts* fame, says, "I have a new ambition. When I get big, I'd like to be a baseball umpire." Charlie Brown asks, "What in the world makes you think you could be a good baseball umpire?" With head high, Lucy replies, "Because I'm always right!"

Excessive talking, which may or may not be compulsive, is another way to avoid listening. Sometimes it is an attempt to divert the conversation from an unwelcome subject. Who has not seen it?

One of the most frequent problems in marriage is the husband who will not listen. But is the conversation worth listening to? The wife should make sure it is. Small talk may seem entirely too insignificant in contrast with the big ideas that have filled the husband's office hours.

Marriage partners who will not listen are already experiencing a separation of interests. For where there is no dialogue, there is emotional divorce. Would it be too strong to suggest that whenever one mate stops listening to the other, he is guilty of a sort of infidelity? It is in attentive and understanding listening that marriage matures.

Talk is absolutely essential in marriage. It's married strangers who quarrel most readily. Silence may be golden—sometimes. But silence can also kill. Buttoned-up lips too often indicate an unsteady heart. Without verbal spillways the tension inside becomes too great, and tragedy can result. The very first barrier to communication should be a danger signal.

One of the most frequent circuit jammers in the marital communication system is the perfectionist within us. The perfectionist is never on a level with his mate. He has to prove everything he says. Even when he is wrong he is right. He may make a good proofreader, but can you think of a more impossible person to live with? Successful marriage partners early learn to communicate as imperfectionists. The apostle John says, "If we say that we have no sin, we deceive ourselves." 1 John 1:8.

I have learned to my chagrin that good communication is deeply involved in semantics.

You know, of course, what a particular word means to you. But what does it mean to your mate? Brittle relationships can be broken by a troublesome word. Is it asking too much for a husband, instead of resorting to stupid adjectives, to say

Trouble With the Personnel

gently, "Why, yes, I can *see* how *anyone* would misunderstand. But this is what I meant."

When a husband and wife get into heated debate, there is always the temptation to forsake the issue and attack the person. There is a Latin term for it—*ad hominem,* meaning "to the man." There are lawyers who, finding themselves without a case, resort to personal attacks. But let's keep the *ad hominems* out of marriage. It's the personal arrows that fly straightest to the mark and leave the deepest scars.

Many a marital rift can be quickly healed by calmly, quietly, and understandingly talking it over. But remember. A sense of security and a feeling of personal worth—these are the basis for opening doors. There can be no useful communication without them. Talking things over without first reestablishing this interrupted undercurrent of confidence in each other's affections is often useless. Communication without first reaffirming one's affection may only degenerate into defense and justification and accusation. Only when love is first solidly reanchored can there be a basis for understanding.

Tell me, Is your antenna so directed that your companion can receive the message? Is yours a relaxed attitude—an environment that encourages talking it over? There may be a torrent of words. But if there is not an attitude of confidence and respect and willingness to listen to the other side with the possibility that it may even be the right side, there is no real communication.

"I love you." These are hard words to say in a moment of tension and misunderstanding. But we need to say them. And we may need to add three words even harder to say—"I was wrong." There are times when a heart cannot be healed without those words. No wonder that the apostle James wrote,

"Confess your faults one to another, and pray one for another, that ye may be healed." James 5:16.

You ask, "What does confession have to do with healing?"

Simply this. We are fast learning that fear, anger, resentment, and bitterness not only lay the groundwork for divorce, but actually poison the body system. Fussing one's way to the divorce court may lead also to the hospital. The body is not made for hate. Body, mind, and soul are made for happiness.

We need to remember that a marital rift, with the scars it has left on mind and body, is healed more easily with words of honest confession than with gifts. In fact, one of the serious delusions of our day is the notion that hearts can be mended with material things. We seem to be caught up in a feverish rush to acquire more and more in the elusive hope of finding happiness and understanding therein.

A few years ago a huge floor-covering corporation featured a delightful ad with all the color and modern appeal of design. Across the ad in striking, bold letters were these words: "Lay linoleum and have a happy home!"

Do you see? Too often when there is home trouble, we think we can heal it if we *lay linoleum.* If there is quarreling or bickering, *lay linoleum.* If the children are wild and disobedient, *lay linoleum.* No. Laying linoleum—or wall-to-wall carpet for that matter, installing a deepfreeze, or contracting for a second automobile—however useful or pleasant, is not the secret of a lasting marriage.

Too many homes are trying to substitute things for words, responsibility for romance, tolerance for love—and hoping the world will never guess!

Dr. Louis Evans draws a fascinating lesson from a detail little noticed in the story of ancient Israel. You can read it in 1

Trouble With the Personnel

Kings 14. Solomon, in the days of his glory, had made "three hundred shields of beaten gold." Then Solomon died, and the glory of the kingdom perished with him.

In the days of Rehoboam, son of Solomon, we read that Shishak, leader of the enemy hosts, "took away all the shields of gold which Solomon had made."

What should they do now? The glory had faded. But Rehoboam determined that the world should never know. He would keep up appearances. He gave the order to make as many shields of brass and shine them until they glittered as pure gold. With these they were to parade bravely and unfalteringly.

"In many a home," says Dr. Evans, "the golden shields of romance have been stolen; the thievery of time or drabness or selfishness or treason or coldness have walked away with the golden shields of romance and rich newness. Marriage is no longer a parade, it is a sullen march."—*Your Marriage—Duel or Duet?* page 123.

How is it in your home, friend? Are you bravely parading with highly polished shields of brass, when they might have been—might still be—shields of pure gold?

What of those who watch the parade? Is your home a convincing demonstration of happiness wall to wall? Do friends and neighbors covet its secret?

And what of the children, the teen-agers who are a part of that home? What does it look like from the inside? Gold? Or brass? Do they consider it the genuine thing? Or only a careless copy? Are they using it as a pattern for their own interpersonal relationships? Are they planning to borrow its blueprint for homes of their own? Or are they left to solve the teen-age dilemma with shields of brass, a heritage of make-believe?

There is no more important question.

5.

Teen-age Dilemma

A LOVABLE and bewildered generation has squandered all its persuasiveness to gain its freedom—but isn't quite sure what to do with it. That is the teen-age dilemma!

What is this new freedom doing to the home? What is it doing to the teen-ager? Can the generation gap be bridged? Is it possible to span the stormy transition from yesterday's dependence to today's independence without catastrophe? God help our homes if we do not discover the answer—in time!

By the time the ink is dry on this page it will be out of date. Circumstances and cultures, fads and fashions, the "ins" and the "outs" are changing faster than they can be evaluated. As I write these words, the hippie movement is beginning to weaken, LSD has begun to decline, abuse of even more dangerous drugs is up, meditation with an Eastern flavor is in, protest is a burning fuse. This is a generation of change—a generation on the move—a generation of pace, passion, and panic. Rebellion is its nature. Protest is its voice. Riot is its anger. Freedom is its possession. The homes of tomorrow are in its hands.

Today's teen-agers are committed to a strange, exploding rebellion that is determined to experiment with life in its own way, with no strings attached. They are a torrent of talent that

Teen-age Dilemma

is going somewhere but hasn't made up its mind. Can the thunderstorm in young hearts be tamed? That is the question.

I write this at the beginning of a long, hot summer. And something tells me we haven't seen anything yet! There will be sit-ins and lie-ins, pickets and protests, marches and counter-marches. Lives will be lost. And we shall not be able to stand aside with our pious pronouncements. We shall be involved whether we like it or not. It is understand—or perish!

Nonviolence, laudable as it is, may be about to expire before our eyes. And ours is not to condemn, but rather to question why. Could it be that we, by our criticism, our condemnation, our lack of understanding, have been guilty of a kind of violence too? Would we be so quick to condemn the marches and the riots—the smoldering of the inner cities—if we knew what is back of this evolution of hate? Are we afraid that to understand would be to condone? It need not be.

It is easy to blame the widespread rioting on university campuses to a small group of militants. But would such radical elements be able to stir up a flame if there were no smoldering embers? Must there not be widespread student dissatisfaction before such protests find sympathy?

Is it possible that faculty and administration have long since lost contact with these students? Are these youth perhaps rebelling against having become just a number? May they not be rebelling against a blind, distant, uncommunicative, faceless authority that makes little attempt to understand?

Like it or not, there is a generation gap. We shall either understand it or perish in its wideness. It need not be condoned, but it cannot be ignored. It must be bridged. For today's offbeat generation will soon be in control, and it will build tomorrow's homes.

Teen-agers say they are tired of being typed, classified, ignored, experimented with, manipulated. They want to be recognized as individuals with individual problems. And they want, most of all, to be accepted as honest.

If you want to know what the kids really think, you might listen to some of the songs they sing. We can then wash our hands and clean our ears and aloofly condemn the undiluted foolishness of the new generation. Or we can, even in their songs, find the telltale words that only thinly disguise a plea for understanding. Words like *deny, defy, simplify, classify*. These are words that come to the top in teen-age thinking. You wouldn't want to be denied, defied, simplified, classified, would you? Teen-agers don't either. But isn't this what they think we are doing to them?

Are we aware of the rattle of the traditional walls? The teen-ager knows that times and tempers are changing. And if his personal dilemma brings perplexity to his elders, it brings panic to himself—underneath the casual exterior.

He is starting out on a perilous journey. And he knows it. He will be responding either to pressure or to purpose. But he doesn't want any interference. He wants to walk the tightrope himself. He wants to learn his own lessons, take his own spills, make his own decisions, meet his own challenges.

He doesn't care for the "Tootle-the-Engine" treatment. Tootle the Engine is a children's story about a young engine named Tootle who went to engine school and was taught two things—to stay on the track and to stop at a red flag. If he always did these things, he would grow up to be a streamliner.

Tootle, being of an inquisitive nature, liked to leave the tracks and go out into the fields to smell the flowers. Finally red flags were placed all through the fields, so that he could

Teen-age Dilemma

not leave the track anywhere without confronting a red flag. You can just hear someone saying, "Stay on the track, Tootle, my boy. Don't ask questions. Don't investigate. Don't argue with the big engines. Just stay on the track, and you'll grow up to be a nice streamliner."

And Tootle Teen-ager absolutely rebels at the sight of red flags!

The teen-ager does not respond to a parade of don'ts. Yet inwardly he craves guidance. His dilemma is twofold. On one hand he resents the spineless lack of authority and restriction in his family. On the other, he rebels at any infraction of his freedom. And so secretly he searches for example. He wants someone to follow.

Teen-agers want a solid, unchanging standard to which they can adjust. But where will they find it? Their parents can hardly appeal to the Ten Commandments, for they themselves, too many of them, have cast them aside. And so, unfortunately, the older generation has long since lost its halo in the eyes of many a youth. Too often there is inconsistency. And one thing a teen-ager finds difficult to tolerate is hypocrisy and pretense. Dare we say he does not find it?

Kids today are weaned on TV. They are pampered. They never had it so good. They are too young to remember the Depression. They can't remember a generation of want. They can't understand adult concern for a livelihood. Our dependence on material things has for them the ring of phoniness. They think it is *our* sense of values that needs changing. Can you blame them?

You see, from the time they are toddlers, in some of the best homes, kids are taught to lie and to break laws. Dad boasts about cheating on his income tax—in the presence of

Jimmy. Mom asks four-year-old Nancy to watch for a cop because she wants to make a U-turn. Is it surprising that the religion of their parents doesn't make sense?

And so, if your teen-age son says, "Dad, I think religion is for the birds," you can do one of two things. You can react with a storm of white-robed denunciation that only further blocks communication. Or you can ask yourself, "What does my boy see in me that makes him think my religion is phony?" And then patiently, without rising temperature—and, believe me, this is an achievement—you can explain how it is that religion makes sense to you—and hope that your example is no block to understanding.

The teen-ager, I say, looks for example. But if deprived of any clearly marked path, he will follow the crowd. He wants to belong. This is the heart cry of the teen-ager. And if that heart cry is not satisfied in the home, where else can he turn but to the crowd? He may simply be rebelling against a generation that didn't care. It might not be so much their moral values that he rejects as it is their lack of caring. And so conformity becomes the greatest propelling force in his life— conformity to the crowd.

You can see that this newly won freedom has its own chains. For many a youth has escaped from society only to be ruled by the crowd. And he finds the one no more charitable, no more flexible, than the other.

Now if conformity involved nothing more than haircuts and jackets and innocent teen vocabulary, there would be no problem. But, unfortunately, the law of public approval demands more than that. Today's teen-ager may think he is not conforming. He may try to be as different as he can. But he is only changing copybooks. He is conforming to the noncon-

Teen-age Dilemma

formists. It is conformity just the same.

Most of us are somewhat familiar with the writings of Bruce Barton. But his father, William B. Barton, in the colorful language of another generation, wrote something worth hearing. Listen!

"We sojourned in Egypt, I and Keturah, and we rode on donkeys, and also on camels. Now, of all the beasts that ever were made, the camel is the most ungainly and preposterous, and also the most picturesque. And he taketh himself very seriously.

"And we beheld a string of five camels that belonged in one caravan, and they were tethered every one to the camel in front of him. But the foremost of the camels had on a halter that was tied to the saddle of a donkey. And I spake unto the man of Arabia who had the camels, and inquired of him how he managed it.

"And he said, 'Each camel followeth the one in front and asketh no questions, and I come after and prod up the last camel.' And I said, 'Doth not the first camel consider that there is no other in front of him, but only an ass?"

"And he answered, 'Nay, for the first camel is blind, and knoweth only that there is a pull at his halter. And every other camel followeth as he is led, and I prod up the hindermost one.' And I inquired, 'How about the donkey?'

"And he said, 'The donkey is too stupid to do anything but keep straight on, and he hath been often over the road.' And I said unto Keturah, 'Behold a picture of human life, for on this fashion have the processions of the ages largely been formed. For there be few men who ask otherwise than how the next in front is going, and they blindly follow, each in the track of those who have gone before.'

"And Keturah said, 'But how about the leader?' And I said, 'That is the profoundest secret of history; for often he who seemed to be the leader was really behind the whole procession.'"

Need I comment?

Yes, conformity has no rival as a driving force in the life of the youth of today. This can be good, I say. Or it can be bad. There are youth today who are challenged to a dedication unsurpassed by any previous generation. But this is not always the case. A brief look at some of our inner cities tells another story.

Consider the slum areas of New York, where teen-agers are forced into gangs against their will. Where the switchblade rules. Where they themselves do not dare to cross the territory of rival gangs. Where life consists of three things—dope, fighting, and sex. Where the little people nine and ten and twelve carry the same kind of guns and knives as their older brothers and sisters and do not use them as sparingly.

What will happen when these little people become teen-agers—and then parents themselves?

And what will happen to the very little people—the babies born to the addicts? Sometimes they go for days without attention. Their mothers may forget where they left them, or may just forget to come home because they are high on heroin. These tots may be left alone in an empty apartment all day long, sitting side by side silently on the bed, afraid to move or speak. What will happen when they are big enough to get downstairs to the streets?

Remember the words of Isaiah 49:15? "Can a woman forget her . . . child? . . . yea, they may forget, yet will I not forget thee."

Teen-age Dilemma 57

The despair on the streets of New York is beyond words. "They're just a bunch of animals," said a cop on the beat. "They ought to be kept in cages, only we don't have enough cages!"

"I don't think Christ would agree with you," said a young Christian worker.

At that the policeman lost his patience. "What would Christ be doing on a street like this?" he shouted.

Somehow I believe that is just where Christ would be— where the need is. But it would be difficult, even for Christ, to make love understood on the city streets. Said one boy, "Jesus didn't know any guys like me when He talked about forgiveness."

I may have talked with that boy. For it was my privilege recently, with my son and one of his friends, to visit the Teen Challenge Center in the heart of Brooklyn where David Wilkerson is doing such an effective work for the boys and girls of the slums. I talked with some of his boys. A new and tragic world seemed to be opening before me.

On one occasion Dave was invited to accompany a group of junkies to a rooftop and watch them "shoot it up." He saw several of the boys injecting heroin into the bloodstream with the same dirty needle. The sight made him pass out cold. The next thing he knew he was lying on the roof.

"Hey, preacher, are you chicken?" one of the boys asked. "Why in the world don't you find a cure?"

The boys laughed. "Where have you been, preacher? We've been to hospitals, we've been to clinics, we've been to doctors, we've seen head shrinkers, we've been hypnotized." One of them clutched his sleeve as he left the roof, looked him straight in the eye, and said, "There are only three ways out—

either OD [overdose], suicide, or God!"

We shudder—and blame it to poverty. Unfortunately, that is not all the picture. The same problems of addiction and other forms of delinquency exist among the wealthier classes of the suburbs. The difference is that kids in the slums are arrested, while those in the suburbs are defended by expensive lawyers (hired by their parents) and let go with nothing more than a scolding.

In one case the youngsters had driven their sports cars across lawns, uprooting the shrubs. Windows were broken, walls smeared with paint, lights and plaster smashed with sledge hammers, paneling hacked away by hatchets.

Who did it? Bored, frustrated rich kids. Said one of the fathers, "They were only letting off steam." Some steam, wouldn't you say—about $400,000 worth!

Is it any wonder that some parents have lost their halo?

The judge said to one boy, son of a noted lawyer, "Young man, do you remember your father, that father whom you have disgraced?"

"I remember him well," the young man replied. "When I went to him for advice or companionship, he would say, 'Run away, boy, can't you see I am busy reading?' Well, Your Honor, my father finished reading his book, and here I am."

Recording this potent testimony makes me look back over the years and desperately wish that I had spent more time with my boys. In fact, is it ever possible to spend too much time with them?

Extreme cases, you say? Isolated? Certainly not typical? I wonder. We might be surprised if we knew what goes on inside some unsuspecting walls.

We recoil from the slums. But the suburbs are not clean.

Teen-age Dilemma

Bill Davidson writes in *The Saturday Evening Post* (May 18, 1968) about the billion-dollar scandal of teen-age shoplifting. More than half of the shoplifters today are teen-agers, most of them white, most of them from middle-class suburban families—and most of them girls. Why do they steal? Just for thrills. It's a game called "beat the system."

It's all a part of today's rebellion against the adult world. Teenagers can't bear to be "square." And they consider shoplifting safer than drugs and less radical than the hippie life.

One girl left a store looking as if she had gained fifteen pounds.. No wonder. She was wearing twelve of the store's bikini bathing suits, one on top of another, under her clothing. Two girls in Beverly Hills tried to leave a store with sixty dollars' worth of blouses. When they resisted arrest, they were handcuffed. And one of them sobbed, "That wasn't a very cool thing to do to us. Why, they treated us like *criminals.*" Often the girls will say, "But, lady, I'll put back the stuff I took. Don't tell me I'm going to be arrested for shoplifting?"

To these teen-agers it's just another way to rebel, another way of saying, "I'm not obeying the rules." And it's a bid for attention. These thrill thieves are really saying to their parents, *"Now* I'll get you to pay attention to me!"

Again I ask, Do you think these are isolated cases? In a department store in the San Fernando Valley, near Los Angeles, it took two hours for a policeman to arrive to pick up a teen-age shoplifter. He apologized for the delay. He had been busy with twenty-six other arrests that afternoon in that one shopping center!

One judge rates this epidemic of shoplifting worse than juvenile crime in the ghettos. But it's a hushed-up American scandal. Permissive parents look the other way.

Yes, permissive parents not only *look* the other way, they sometimes *point* the other way. More than apathy, and more than shoplifting, is wrong with the modern home. Billy Graham tells of a college girl who was fatally injured in a car accident. Her last words to her mother were these: "Mother, you taught me everything I needed to know to get by in college. You taught me how to light my cigarette, how to hold my cocktail glass, and how to have intercourse safely. But, Mother, you never taught me how to die. You better teach me quickly, Mother, because I'm dying."

Can America long stand with homes like these as its foundation? We've come a long way, haven't we, since the early chapters of this book where we talked of the ideal.

From childhood we have been taught to honor motherhood. But does the fact of motherhood—of fatherhood—change the character? The slum children of today, the sophisticated rich kids of today, will be the parents of tomorrow. *And there may not be any miracle between!*

It is evident that we dare not be too quick to blame youth for its problems. For the older generation, with its own moorings upset, with its own goals confused, must take its share of responsibility. Back of youth's blurred image is a lack of restraint on the part of well-meaning parents.

This headline met my eye recently: "Sorry, kids. We now know that the strictest parents have the happiest children."

Yes, youth want help. They want guidance. They want restriction. They want love that cares enough to set some rules. They want consistent example. But too often these are lacking. In a shocking number of cases there is no real communication between parents and youth. And advice from professional sources is too often only meaningless rationalization of

Teen-age Dilemma

what is taking place. Listen to what a professor in a church-related college told a group of students:

"Neither rape nor incest, nor any other sexual act, nor indeed the denial of one's Lord or the violation of the First Commandment by having another god, is necessarily and always wrong."

Strange accommodation! The new morality, they call it. Says one educator, "This is the morality which has conquered the college world today; it is *less than half a generation* from becoming the standard ethics of our nation." (Emphasis supplied.)

The new morality? No, it's the old immorality!

The teen-agers know what to call it. I doubt if ever they seriously overstep the bounds of the Ten Commandments without hearing conscience speak. Morality has been repressed. It has been pushed aside. But it is still there. Conscience still echoes, even though faintly, the insistent "thou shalt not" of Sinai.

Have I painted too discouraging a picture of our nation's morals? I am not so sure. But thankfully there is another side. It is possible to find among youth of today, a dedication unsurpassed by any previous generation. There are thousands of parents who *are* living before their children a consistent example, without pretense or sham. There is an army of teen-agers who, living in the very shadow of today's moral letdown, remain untainted.

I picked up a copy of *Morals '68* the other day and found this comment by Harry Ferguson: "What we have to keep in mind is that persons who are committing what we consider to be immoral acts are always in the minority. If you lumped together all the pornographers, . . . prostitutes, drug pushers and drug takers, hate groups of both the left and right, hippies, burglars, swindlers, and dishonest politicians or policemen, the total probably would not reach 10 million."—Page 6.

I was encouraged when I read this. Ten million. And there are 200 million Americans. But then I read on:

"What about the morals of the 190 million other Americans—the great backbone of the nation? They are not perfect, of course. Some of them commit adultery, steal from the supermarket, engage in malicious gossip, drink too much, drive too fast, and fall into debt beyond their means. But it is not those things that worry historians and sociologists. It is mounting evidence that the average American is becoming apathetic toward the real values of life."

It is this apathy, this indifference, that gnaws at the moral fiber of this generation. It is this apathy that is passed on to the teen-age world, where it smolders into anything from confusion to open revolt.

Teen-agers want help. Are we in a position to give it to them?

We try. But could it be that counselors of youth today are making a serious mistake—in fact two serious mistakes? One is the notion that changing times demand changing moral standards. Those holding this view insist that conscience is answerable only to public opinion. On the other hand, there are those counselors who attempt to hold back the flood of immorality, but who have no weapon except strict self-discipline to set against it. And self-discipline alone, without Christ, won't work.

There is only one power strong enough to hold a young man or a young woman, a boy or a girl, in the hour of temptation. It is the power of the living Christ. What a man needs is not self-discipline alone, but a Saviour. He needs a miracle. He

Teen-age Dilemma

needs a promise like this: "Sin shall not have dominion over you." Romans 6:14.

The dominion of sin, the grip of evil over mind and body—this is the chain that needs to be broken. This is the captivity from which man needs release. And he is helpless except for the power of the conquering Christ.

I realize, of course, that even self-discipline is going out of fashion. Instead, love is said to be the final arbiter in any situation. And love, if you handle it right, can be made to excuse a moral failure in the first place. Why do you need self-control; why do you need the keeping power of Christ if what yesterday was sin—and what you know deep in your heart is still sin—is now said to be only a meaningful relationship? Do you see why the new generation is confused? Desperately confused?

Love, they say, is the answer. But is love to measure itself by itself? Is love to have no guidelines? Are ethical standards to be decided by the emotion of the moment? Is love no longer responsible to law? Does love lie—and steal—and kill—and commit adultery—sometimes? Is crime sanctified by calling it love?

Says David Redding, "Stretching morals to suit this plastic predicament is what is meant by the New Morality, and that brings us immediately to its problem. Telling a susceptible teen-ager, headed for the back seat of a car, to 'love the meaningful' may not be sufficiently explicit to meet the practical pressures of her temptation. In advance, she must know when and where she is going to say No, or be at the mercy of subjective emotion that may scar her permanently. Without the strategy of being guided in advance by commandments, conscience itself is footloose in the heat of battle."—*The New Immorality,* page 13.

Love needs some guidelines. Said Jesus, "If ye love Me, keep My commandments." John 14:15.

Tell me. That giant bridge that you cross frequently. Have you ever driven into the guardrail as you crossed? Do you know anybody who has?

What would happen if there were no guardrails? "Oh," you say, "I would drive off the edge!"

Probably not. Not necessarily. The bridge would still be as wide. But you like the security of the guardrails, just to be sure.

These guardrails, you see, are like the commandments of God, placed there for our security and protection. They keep us within certain limits. No one suggests that the rails on the bridge should be removed, that they restrict our freedom. No one tries to crash into them. No one tries to see how close to the edge he can drive. We keep a safe distance. Love, too, needs some guardrails. Love needs defining. Otherwise it may too easily be confused with emotion, with the insistent pull of desire in the moment of temptation.

I know that these pages will be held in the hands of youth across the continent—from Maine to Saskatchewan, from Los Angeles to New York. You are the husbands and wives of tomorrow. You hold tomorrow's homes in the power of your decision.

Did you know that contentment on the part of your mate, on the part of your children, depends very much on the trustworthiness developed long before the wedding day? You see, he who is a nomad before marriage will likely be a nomad after marriage. The roving eye will not easily learn to hold its gaze steady. A habit of polygamy before marriage may perpetuate itself later. It takes more than the fanfare of a big wedding to

Teen-age Dilemma 65

break habits established by long practice.

We smile at what a small boy wrote about King David. But it's dead serious. He said, "David was a good and rich king. If there was anything wrong with him, it was a slight tendency to adultery."

The church is not out to scotch romance. Rather, it wants to keep you from being cheated out of the real thing. Said the apostle, "Now unto Him that is able to do exceeding abundantly above all that we ask or think." Ephesians 3:20.

Again from David Redding: "Teen-agers do have to be different from their parents to prove they are becoming independent, but they should choose constructive ways to rebel. Why hurt yourself simply to show mother that the apron strings are stretching? Go your parents one better. If you feel compelled to oppose them, do so on grounds other than immorality, or you and your future home will have to take the beating. If you really want to shock your folks, go into the ministry! You can be different without being destructive."—*The New Immorality,* pages 40, 41.

You hold tomorrow, I say, in the power of your decision—whatever that decision may be.

Youth, you see, are at liberty to decide what they will do with the freedom they have won. Some will squander it. Some will disgrace it. But an army will march with honest pride in the parade of today's youthful heroes.

While youth are burning their draft cards, dozens of medics, in the tradition of Desmond Doss, are walking unarmed into the keenest dangers of war, their one purpose to save life.

While enemy cities are being bombed, mission pilots like Clyde Peters, in many lands, are flying their errands of mercy close between mountains, touching down on short, muddy airstrips—because there are lives to be saved, bodies to be healed.

While the big cities count their runaway kids in the thousands, and while bewildered mothers walk the streets looking for their children, teen-agers in some lands are being disowned by their parents, pushed out of their homes because they have acknowledged the claims of their Lord.

While long lines of youth are marching for causes hardly commendable, other groups, equally enthusiastic, are touring the nation with their "Up With People" spectacular, singing out their dedication and polishing the image of youth with their wholesomeness.

Yes, while restless teens are rioting in the streets, or holding aloft the defiant placards of some unworthy protest, others are displaying their colors in the pageant of the heroes, the parade of the free.

What will youth do with the freedom it has won? That is the teen-age dilemma. But thousands have discovered the answer in the words of a simple prayer:

> Make me a captive, Lord,
>   And then I shall be free;
> Force me to render up my sword;
>   And I shall conqueror be.

Could any storm destroy a home built upon such a surrender to the claims of Christ? Hardly!

6.
Bribing the Gatekeeper

MANY years ago a Chinese emperor built a gigantic wall to defend the country against the barbarians to the north. The wall stretched for miles along the border, and it was wide enough for chariots to pass on its top. It remains one of the wonders of the world, and it may be the one man-made object that will be visible from the moon. But as a defense effort, the wall was a complete failure. *The enemy breached it by merely bribing a gatekeeper!*

The fiercest, toughest, most decisive battle ever fought is the battle for the mind. It is the mind that decides. It is the mind that chooses. It is the mind that loves. It is the mind that worships. It is the mind that is tempted. The mind is the fortress of the soul. The Creator has built its defenses strong. *But He has made you the gatekeeper.*

What are the weapons in this battle? Words. Billions of words arranged into advertising, crowded into newspapers, bound into books. Words in the air. Words on the screen. Words on the lips of friends or enemies. Words of husbands and wives. Subtle changers of the mind that scar and mold and enslave. Words endlessly repeated. Cutting grooves into the consciousness of willing or unwilling listeners. Shaping characters. And shaping homes.

It was during the Korean War that an American Marine officer, Colonel Frank Schwable, was taken prisoner by the Chinese Communists. And it was not long before it dawned on him that the enemy expected to use him as a tool of propaganda.

The weeks pass. He suffers rough, inhuman treatment, intimidation, hunger, interrogation for hours on end. He will be better treated, he is told, if he will just unburden himself of guilt. What guilt, he wonders. But soon he finds out. Over the weeks there is a slowly induced hypnosis, and at last, after months of intense psychological pressure, he signs a "confession" that the United States is carrying on germ warfare against the enemy. He gives details.

He said later, "That is the hardest thing I have to explain: how a man can sit down and write something he knows is false, and yet, to sense it, to feel it."

Time, fear, and continual pressure—and never-ending words—had created a menticidal hypnosis. And it could happen to anyone!

A prominent psychiatrist, testifying in the Schwable case, stated that nearly anybody under such circumstances could be forced to sign a similar confession.

"Anyone in this room?" he was asked.

He looked about at the officers sitting in judgment and replied firmly, "Anyone in this room!"

The techniques of brainwashing are becoming more and more precise. The days of witchcraft and torture and the rack may have passed. But the modern refinements of these are here to stay. It is no longer simply a battle for man's body. It is a battle for the mind.

The military aspects, the military possibilities, of such war-

Bribing the Gatekeeper 69

fare are frightening. Mass brainwashing, mass hypnotism, and drug warfare could subdue whole nations without firing a shot. It is said that a single pound of LSD scattered in the water supply of New York City, with supporting doses, could mentally incapacitate its population long enough for an invading army to take over.

But it is not only the military possibilities that should stagger us. The sweeping hysteria of suggestion is invading the home every day by way of television, radio, and the printed page. We are subjected to a barrage of suggestion, a bombardment of ideas that is slowly conditioning us in areas of life that affect our destiny. And I am not referring to simple advertising.

What we are witnessing is the battle for the mind. More than that, it is the battle for the will of man. And it is a battle for the home.

In every encounter with the forces of evil the battle is fought first, and won or lost, in the mind, before friends or family know it. If ever a man is disloyal to God, to his country, or to his wife, he is disloyal first in the mind. If, as the gatekeeper, he allows temptation free access to the corridors of the mind, there will be no way of escape from the brainwashing forces that will beat against his imagination. And in any conflict between the will and the imagination, usually the imagination wins. Infidelity is the almost inevitable result. It can happen to anyone—anyone who reads this page.

You say, "Pastor Vandeman, do you mean that a man is helpless against temptation? Like Colonel Schwable?"

No. There is one difference. Colonel Schwable was physically forced to remain under the influence of brainwashing propaganda. You are not. You are the gatekeeper. But if you accept the enemy's bribe, if you choose to open your mind to the repetitious rantings of temptation, broken hearts and broken homes are inevitable.

To tamper with the mind is to tamper with the conscience, with the power to decide, with the will. To control the mind is to control the conscience. The mind must be kept strong. It is the unguarded mind that is open to temptation.

The will is the enemy's target. For the will, you see, is the soul's deciding power. It is your decision. It is your choice. Inclination may be strong. Human nature may be weak. But the will decides. The will is the real you.

The will is free. It was never God's will that it should be otherwise. It was never God's plan that any outside influence should control man's will. God *will not* control it without your invitation. Satan *cannot* control it without your permission. It is man who decides.

God never enters the sacred precincts of the conscience uninvited. Satan would like to enter. Family or friends would sometimes like to enter. But God says to the watching universe, "See that man. He is about to make a decision. By that decision he may live or die. But he alone must make it. Stand back! The soul must be free!"

And God Himself waits in the courtyard, stands at the door and knocks, while man decides.

God paid a terrific price to keep the soul free. That price was the death of His Son. It cost the life of Jesus to preserve for you and me the right to choose. God will never force the will. He will only accept it. He wants only willing allegiance.

The enemy, on the other hand, will use any subterfuge, any hellish device to force the will of man.

And so the battle continues. The enemy wants the will of

Bribing the Gatekeeper

man—to enslave it. God wants the will—to set it free.

What are some of the forces that try to bribe their entry into the mind?

Take hypnotism, for instance. Hypnotism, once regarded as only a harmless parlor game, now comes to us in cap and gown. It professes to free man from undesirable habits. It poses as a great benefactor. But what about the mind? What about the will? When the will is surrendered to another, placed under the control of another, is it not to some extent enslaved and weakened? Is it ever so strong again?

You trust your friend. You trust your counselor. You trust your dentist. But is it ever safe to surrender the will to another? Suppose that in some hypnotic session another intelligence than that of the one you trust should take over. De Witt Miller has put the question this way: "When the subconscious mind, under hypnosis, becomes susceptible to outward suggestions, how can we be sure that some astral interloper of the spirit world will not intrude upon the subconscious mind, in its hypnotic trance-state, and ply its occult arts, as it does with an entranced medium?"—*Reincarnation,* page 37.

It has happened. That is the possibility. That is the danger. Hypnotism is a perilous passkey to the mind. Could it be that hypnotism is delivering on a silver platter what psychic forces have been seeking through the ages—the control of the will?

Is it any wonder that Solomon said, "Keep thy heart [thy mind] with all diligence; for out of it are the issues of life." Proverbs 4:23.

And what of the pills that we swallow by the billions? Are they strengthening the mind, making it more secure against temptation? Or are they subtle bribers at the gate?

Dr. Paul Tournier, the famous Swiss psychiatrist, says,

"Man's need for religion is so great that if the true one is taken from him, he makes up others for himself. There is a religion of the medicine bottle, and there are others, more naive still. It is surprising to see how many strong characters, who reject all recourse to divine help in life's difficulties as being the relic of an outmoded past, fasten their hope of salvation on some drug simply because it is the product of scientific progress. Having been told that this progress has no bounds, that it would make it possible to conquer all disease, men have been imbued with the fallacious hope that, thanks to science, they will be *able to live completely disordered lives with impunity.*"–*The Healing of Persons,* pages 102, 103. (Emphasis supplied.)

You see the philosophy. Live as you please. Then take Brand X. And all the time you are weakening the defenses of the mind.

Robert S. de Ropp, in his book *Drugs and the Mind,* makes this sparkling comment about our pill-taking generation: "Lucky neurotics! Soon the specter of care will be banished from the world, the burden of anxiety and guilt will be lifted from your souls. The restoration of your primeval innocence, your re-entry into the Garden of Eden, will now be accomplished through the agency of a pill. Soothed by reserpine, calmed by chlorpromazine, mellowed by 'Miltown,' elevated by 'Meratran,' what need you fear from the uncertainties of fortune? Tranquilly, smoothly your days will succeed one another, like the waters of a peaceful river flowing through green pastures in which graze dewy-eyed cows whose state of placid contentment resembles your own. O most fortunate of mortals, whose spiritual defects are made good by the skill of the scientist, whose personal shortcomings are supplemented by a formula. No longer need you struggle with your weaknesses or

Bribing the Gatekeeper

agonize over your sins. Salvation need not be purchased at the cost of spiritual war. In the chemopsychiatric age you can buy it by the bottle. O brave new world that has such bottles in it!"—Pages 283, 284.

Would you say we are sharpening the sensitivities of the conscience? Making it stronger? Or weakening it pill by pill?

But all this is nothing compared to the psychedelic whirlpool into which this generation is being drawn. The mind-changing drugs, the consciousness-expanding drugs are sweeping the country. Marijuana, LSD, and Methedrine, which makes even LSD pale by comparison.

Every user of LSD is a potential suicide. One boy felt so free that he thought he was God. And so, convinced that nothing could harm him, he walked into oncoming traffic and was almost killed. Users often get delusions of grandeur. They even think they can fly. A boy in Los Angeles was about to throw his girl friend off the roof when the cops caught him. And the worst of it is that you may freak out again, years later, without repeating the drug. I ask you, is it insight? Or is it insanity?

It is estimated that a billion impulses are being sent to our brain every second. Most of them are shut out, fortunately, from our awareness. Someone has suggested that these mind-changing drugs may be dilating the aperture so that more of the impulses get through. This could explain the chaotic nature of the drug experience. At times impulses may be wired directly to the euphoria center, with all other connections unplugged. In that case everything seems fabulously wonderful. But sometimes the connections are not so wired, and the experience is one of nameless horror. In other words, the drug experience may be a temporary rewiring of the brain circuits!

Think of it, friend! Do you see the danger? Do you see what these psychedelic bribers at the gate are doing? Tampering with the mind. Tampering with the seat of decision. Tampering with the conscience. Tampering with a man's eternal destiny!

Is it any wonder that some observers are now speaking of the total annihilation of the will of man?

How jealously we should guard the will! For every influence, every impression allowed entrance to the mind, is shaping the set of the will, determining its future choices and affecting the destiny.

Every time we decide right, we are strengthening the will. And every time we decide wrong, we are weakening the will. It's as simple as that. It may be a little thing, a small decision —as seemingly insignificant as a second piece of pie. But we are either weakening or strengthening the will by that decision. Habits, good or bad, are being strengthened by exercise.

We are wise when we beware of anything that dulls the power of the will. Alcohol can do it. Tobacco can do it. Overeating can do it. Fatigue can do it.

Now someone is saying, "Pastor Vandeman, you're talking about me. I know what I ought to do. But I have absolutely no will power."

That is the cry of thousands of alcoholics. No will power! And a legion of smokers echo it. No will power! It is the plaintive cry of millions of weight watchers who put off their weight watching until tomorrow. And the uncounted victims of temper and lust join in. No will power! It is a cry of defeat that makes the heart of God weep.

I think you can see how intensely practical this is. It is not sufficient to talk to an alcoholic about exercising his will,

Bribing the Gatekeeper

strengthening his will. For he says hopelessly, "I have none!"

Friend, if we must tie our hopes to our own weakness, or to man-made solutions, or to the manipulations suggested by popular psychology, however helpful their insights, there is reason to despair. For what can a man do when the will is weakened? What can a man do when the will is enslaved by a wrong choice in the past?

Listen. There is hope. For weak though a man may be, he still *has* a will. He still has the *power to choose*. He can *reverse* the unwise decision of the past. He can *choose to change masters*. He can *cry out for deliverance!*

An inspired writer has said it so much better than I can: "The expulsion of sin is the act of the soul itself. True, we have no power to free ourselves from Satan's control; but when we desire to be set free from sin, and in our great need cry out for a power out of and above ourselves, the powers of the soul are imbued with the divine energy of the Holy Spirit, and they obey the dictates of the will in fulfilling the will of God."–*The Desire of Ages,* page 466.

What a paragraph! Read it again and again. Every word of it filled with hope!

Yes, there is hope for the most hopeless. Listen. "Sin shall not have dominion over you." Romans 6:14.

Evidently a man doesn't have to be enslaved by habit. Evidently he doesn't have to see his home disintegrating because of his weakness. Evidently God can break the chains. That's what Jesus came to do.

"The Spirit of the Lord is upon Me, because He hath anointed Me . . . to preach deliverance to the captives, and recovering of sight to the blind, to set at liberty them that are bruised." Luke 4:18.

Jesus came to break the chains, to set the captive free. He says in John 8:32: "Ye shall know the truth, and the truth shall make you free."

When we learn the truth about what we are discussing here, it will set us free. Not one person who reads this page needs to remain a slave to crippling habit. Every one of you can go free. I say this on the authority of the Word of the living God. "If the Son therefore shall make you free, ye shall be free indeed." John 8:36.

Again, we need to understand that this decisive victory is not achieved by sheer force of self-discipline—by frantic trying. This is made vividly clear in the story of the Indian fakir who once came to a village declaring he would demonstrate how to make gold. The villagers gathered around as he poured water into a huge cauldron, put some coloring matter into it, and began to repeat mantras as he stirred.

When their attention was temporarily diverted, he let some gold nuggets slip down into the water. Stirring a little more, he finally poured off the water, and there was the gold at the bottom of the cauldron.

The villagers' eyes bulged. The moneylender offered 500 rupees for the formula, and the fakir sold it to him.

"But," the fakir explained, "here is the secret. You must not think of the red-faced monkey as you stir. If you do, the gold will never come."

The moneylender promised to remember that he was to forget. But to try to forget is to remember, as the fakir well knew. So try as hard as he might, the red-faced monkey sat on the edge of the moneylender's mind, spoiling all his gold.

Friend, whatever gets your mind gets you. Whatever captures the imagination will enslave you. You can never cast sin

Bribing the Gatekeeper

out of the mind by trying to forget it. For sin thrives upon attention, even negative attention. Even a loyal attempt to fight sin in the mind can lead to defeat. Do you see now why the sheer force of self-discipline is not enough—why frantic trying doesn't work?

Yes. You cannot control your thoughts and your feelings and your emotions as you may desire. But there is one thing you can do. You can control your will. You can choose who your master shall be. Joshua said, "Choose you this day whom ye will serve." Joshua 24:15.

And that is an act of the will. We choose our master. It will be one—or it will be the other. Every man is under the control of one power or the other—by deliberate choice.

Do you see the constant peril a man is in until he understands the true force of the will? The will is not something to be pushed about by circumstances, or smothered under feelings, or intimidated by habit or impulse. It need not be subject to the emotions. The life of victory is not to be lived in the emotions, but in the will.

This desire may pull in one direction. This emotion may pull in another. This habit, this temper, this lust may clamor for attention. But the will decides. And the will is the real you.

God does not negotiate with the feelings. He negotiates with the will. In the final destiny of man the feelings are not the deciding factor. It is the will that decides. Let the emotions rebel as they may. They will gradually come into line with the decision of the will. It is yours to decide. And when you do, the power of God, like the lift of the tide, will make all the difference!

I think of the building of a giant bridge across a portion of New York's harbor. Engineers were searching for a base upon which to rest one of the mighty buttresses.

But deep in the mud and practically buried, they discovered an old barge, full of bricks and stones, that had long ago sunk to that spot. It had to be moved. Yet in spite of every device it remained firmly held to its muddy bed.

At last one of the engineers conceived an idea. He gathered other barges about and secured them by long chains to the sunken wreck *while the tide was low.* Then all waited. The tide was coming in. Higher and higher rose the water, and with it the floating barges. Then creaking and straining on the chains, that old boat was lifted from its viselike grip—raised by the lift of the Atlantic Ocean!

Need I draw a parallel?

I ask you, Is your mind like an old barge full of bricks and stones, gripped by memories you long to forget, held by age-long leanings and habits you would give anything to be released from, bound by fears and uncontrolled imaginations? Has every human device failed to break the power of their viselike grip in your life? Just know that the lift of the mighty God will deliver you. He is able. But you must choose.

The enemy of God and man is not willing that this priceless secret be clearly understood. For he knows that when you receive it fully, his power will be broken. You will be free—and your home secure!

7.

When the Rain Falls

A YOUNG man and his father farmed a small piece of land. Several times a year they would load up a cart with vegetables and take them to market.

The two had little in common. The son was a tense and ambitious individual, the go-getter type. The father, on the other hand, was steady and relaxed.

One morning they loaded the cart, hitched up the ox, and started out for the nearest city. The young man, true to his disposition, kept prodding the ox with a stick. He reasoned that they had a better chance of getting good prices if they reached the marketplace early.

Several hours down the road the father stopped. It was his brother's farm, and he wanted to say hello, for so seldom did he have the opportunity. The son, of course, was impatient at what he considered a needless delay, and did not conceal his restlessness. But the father cautioned, "Take it easy. You'll last longer."

After an hour they drove on. They came to a fork in the road and the father turned to the right. "The other way is shorter," the son reminded him. "Yes, Son. But this way is more beautiful."

"Have you no respect for time?"

"Yes," said the father, "I respect it so much that I like to use it in looking at beautiful things."

At twilight they found themselves in country as lovely as a garden. The father suggested, "Let's sleep here." By this time the boy was angry, and he exploded, "You're more interested in flowers than money!"

But the father quietly replied, "That's the nicest thing you've said in a long time."

"I'll never take a trip with you again!" the boy vowed.

In the morning they were on their way early. Soon they came upon a cart in the ditch, and the father stopped to help while the son, of course, protested. "Take it easy," said the father. "Sometime you might be in the ditch yourself."

And then it was eight o'clock. There was a brilliant flash of lightning. And thunder. "Must be a big rain in the city," said the old man.

"But, Dad, if we had hurried, we could have been sold out by now."

"Take it easy, Son. You'll last longer."

It was late afternoon when they reached the hill overlooking the city. The two men stood for a long moment, looking down. Neither said a word.

And then the son broke the silence. "I see what you mean, Father."

They turned and drove their cart away from what had been, until eight o'clock that morning, *the city of Hiroshima!*

It was not long after the explosion of that first atomic bomb that Bob Ripley originated a broadcast from the ill-fated city. And I heard him say, "I am standing on the spot where the end of the world began!"

Time is running out. We live our days under the ticking of a

When the Rain Falls

universal time-fuse. For a generation now we have lived in an atmosphere of tension that is on the verge of hysterics. The tension tolerance of humanity is reaching the breaking point.

We have permitted ourselves to be stampeded into unnatural and dangerous pressures. We hate to miss a single panel of a revolving door. We have compressed our lives into high-speed capsules. We pay with a terrific toll. And it is telling on our homes.

Is there a way to live in this kind of world serenely? How much can we stand? Can these bodies, these minds, these homes take the tensions into which we have been thrust? We live in a broken world. Is it possible to be a whole person in a broken world? Is it possible to relax when the rain falls, and the thunder crashes round our heads? How can we deal with stress in the mind, in the body, in the home?

It was back in 1925 that a young medical student at the University of Prague, burning with enthusiasm for the art of healing, noticed what many physicians before him had noticed, that certain symptoms are common to a great many diseases, and are therefore of little help in making diagnosis. For instance, the fact that a patient feels somewhat ill, has a slight fever, a loss of appetite, and a few scattered aches and pains, would hardly enable a physician to pinpoint the disease.

Young Hans Selye was too new in the medical profession to realize just how laughable his question might sound to his elders—if he should find the courage to ask it. But why, he wondered, had physicians since the dawn of medicine given their attention to understanding the specific symptoms of individual diseases and never troubled themselves to understand the condition of just being sick?

What is it that makes a man sick—not sick with pneumonia,

or sick with scarlet fever, or sick with measles, but just plain sick? Why could not the methods and instruments of research be applied to that problem?

That question in a pioneering young mind was the beginning of a lifetime of research that has resulted in a most valuable contribution to mankind—the better understanding of the stress of life.

Stress, you see, is simply the wear and tear of life. It is what life does to you. Stress is not necessarily caused by some great problem that rolls suddenly upon the mind or body of man. It may be caused by simply crossing a street in traffic, by reading with poor light, by the crying of a baby, by an endless variety of routine everyday occurrences—even by sheer joy.

Now, it is not possible to avoid stress entirely. But it is possible, and very important, to adjust your reaction to it, to strengthen the body's defenses against it. For medical science now knows that many diseases are caused largely by errors in the body's response to stress, rather than by germs or poisons or any other outside agent.

One of Dr. Selye's most valuable, and yet disturbing, contributions has been to point out that every man begins life with a certain reserve of vital force. Once it is gone, it cannot be replaced. It is like a bank account that can be depleted by withdrawals but cannot be increased by deposits.

Many people use up this vitality, restore it from superficial supplies, and are tricked into thinking the loss has been made up by rest. On the contrary, every withdrawal of the deeper reserves of vital force leaves its scar. Somewhere the defenses are wearing thin.

And neither the body nor the mind can take too much wear in the same place. Thousands are in mental hospitals because

When the Rain Falls

ruts have been worn in the mind. The same thoughts, the same problems, the same fears and frustrations, have worn a groove deeper and deeper until the mind has become unbalanced. The mind could have stood a variety of problems. But not the same one endlessly repeated.

A man's mind is the most elaborate computer ever devised. But it is too delicate to stand the strain of continuous cutting in the same spot. And overloaded minds, like overloaded electrical circuits, have a way of blowing a fuse. Beyond certain endurance levels the mind and body cannot give.

Do you begin to see what happens in some marital relationships?

Dr. H. S. Liddell and Dr. A. V. Moore, Cornell University psychologists, in experiments upon sheep, disclosed that a series of daily unpleasant incidents, applied with repetition, can in time reduce a sheep to a bleating, neurotic animal and can eventually cause its death.

Let me remind you again of the words of the late Dr. John Schindler: "Most cases of emotionally induced illness are the result of a monotonous drip, drip of ... unpleasant emotions, the everyday run of anxieties, fears, discouragements and longings."—*How to Live 365 Days a Year,* page 13.

The drip-of-the-faucet experience again. How do you—and I—react to stress that has become familiar by long repetition? That is the question.

Remember the father and son—traveling toward Hiroshima? In that simple narrative we find some delightful contrasts that help us understand how to deal with stress.

Here were two men, two types, under the same pressures, both traveling toward Hiroshima. They lived in the same world, in the same home, with circumstances they could not change. But their physical, mental, and spiritual reactions were in contrast.

Both were physically fit. Both worked in the open air. But the father had learned how to relax, how to balance work with rest. The son had not.

Their mental attitudes were opposite. Each had a different set of values.

The father trusted his God. The son permitted only selfishness and ambition to rule his life.

Remember the delay as the father visited with his brother? In the son's way of life there was no time for family or friends —only getting ahead. But how many a man has lost his own family, his wife, his children—lost them to self, to society, and to God—because he was too busy!

Remember the cart in trouble? What a contrast between son and father, between selfishness and selflessness! When will we learn the eroding influence of selfishness? When will we learn that sharing is life-giving?

Listen to the words of God through the ancient prophet: "Is not this the fast that I have chosen? to loose the bands of wickedness, to undo the heavy burdens, and to let the oppressed go free, and that ye break every yoke? Is it not to deal thy bread to the hungry, and that thou bring the poor that are cast out to thy house? when thou seest the naked, that thou cover him?" Isaiah 58:6, 7.

And now notice verse 8: "Then shall thy light break forth as the morning, and thine health shall spring forth speedily."

A tremendous promise! A fantastic promise! Many a man, many a woman, has found health when he turned his attention to helping someone else. There is no influence more healing than the spring of unselfishness flowing from within.

When the Rain Falls

And remember the flowers? The father and the son had a different set of values. The father had wisely learned that we are healingly distracted from the tensions of life by the beauties of nature. But the son was a puppet of his stunted philosophy of life.

How much the son missed! And how much we miss of life's richest rewards! We hurl ourselves into life with such reckless abandon that we wring ourselves physically and spiritually dry. We fasten our eyes on some glittering prize of material success. But when we reach it, if we do, we find that the badge of our success is a stomach ulcer or a thrombosis. Stress has taken its toll. The home has suffered. And it didn't need to be that way!

Said Jesus, "Seek ye first the kingdom of God, and His righteousness; and all these things shall be added unto you." Matthew 6:33.

But now one more parallel in our story. The father and son were traveling toward Hiroshima. They didn't know that the bomb would be dropped at eight o'clock that morning. Was it Providence that kept them from being there at that hour? Was it the father's faith? Perhaps so.

But not all who have trusted have been spared. Some have perished when the bombs fell. Some have been burned at the stake. John the Baptist trusted—and was beheaded.

But friend, here is the point. The father's trust did not depend upon God's sparing him from Hiroshima. The father did not know. He only knew his God. He only knew that whatever God permitted was all right with him. Like the patriarch Job he could say confidently, "Though He slay me, yet will I trust in Him." Job 13:15.

Are you a victim of tension, anxiety, grasping frustration—

like the son? Or is yours a serene, purposeful, selfless confidence—like that of the father? Is your home a picture of tension between father and son, between mother and daughter, or husband and wife? Your home will reflect your own reactions to stress. The way you meet personal stresses and crises and emergencies will be transferred to the family. To keep tension out of the home you must keep it out of the personality.

We may need to remember that, as marriage partners, we can never reach the promised land without going through some wilderness together. And believe me, there will be wilderness. And there will be rain.

It is not necessary to be a practiced diagnostician to see that our world today is not in good health. It is a broken world, a world in deep trouble. War, poverty, and disease are only symptoms. The world is troubled in the spirit.

We are told that every epoch has its own particular malady. The typical sickness of this generation is neurosis. Many doctors agree that more than half their patients suffer from it. And this is not accidental. For our aloof, materialistic, sophisticated society no longer supplies the deeper needs of the soul.

What is neurosis? Simply speaking, a person is neurotic when he represses something without eliminating it. How, then, has neurosis touched this generation? The answer is self-evident. This generation is told so often as to sound convincing that feeling, faith, and Biblical truth are unimportant. Yet men and women at the bottom of their hearts feel a justified intuition that these things are nonetheless important.

Our thirst for love, our spiritual loneliness, our fear of death, the riddle of evil, the mystery of God—we may not speak of these; we may repress them. But they still haunt us. They are repressed but not eliminated. This makes a man sick.

When the Rain Falls

This makes a world sick. For in repressing values without having been freed from them, man has repressed the very principle of inner harmony.

What is the result? Modern man, like the adolescent in profound crisis, turns to strange alien behavior. He turns to the bribers at the gate.

Is it possible to be a whole person in a broken world? Is it possible to have a solidly built home, with happiness wall to wall, in a world like this? Even when the rain falls?

It simply must be so. The alternative is to stand one day beside a broken home and view it as a city in shambles, a relationship beyond repair.

One young woman, looking back upon her broken home, realizing where both partners had made mistakes, recalling how they had listened to the unsound counsel of friends, wrote these words:

"The war is over. We stood just now beside the ruins of our city and used the magic word *forgive*. We understand now. We know now that the city was destroyed by mistake.

"It didn't need to happen. No bomb was dropped upon it. It was carefully built with the best of materials. The voice of prayer was often heard within it. No wonder it had long stood serene and calm against every weapon from without.

"But now it lies in ruins. And we—no one else—we are to blame. You see, we tore it down with words. Your words—my words—words of other people, people who did not understand. But we listened to those words—and began to believe them. And now—.

"We were so foolish. We were like children toppling their toy villages. Toppling them with never a care. At first we were afraid. We tried to stop. But one word flamed another until fires broke out in our city that we could not quench. Others were watching now. There were those who liked to see it burn. And then, ignited by hate, our smoldering feelings burst into a final holocaust of words and we abandoned the city.

"We stood beside it just now. The smoking cloud has lifted. Time has cleared our vision. We understand. We forgive. The war is over. But our city is in a shambles. And even forgiveness can never build it again!"

Friend, it need not happen to you or me. Not if we let God teach us the delicate work of mending hearts. Not if we let Him teach us patience and understanding. Not if there is a simple, basic honesty about our own weaknesses—with each other and with God.

Does not the confidence of our mates challenge the best that is in us? I think so. That is why I like the familiar hymn of all churches that says, "I would be true, for there are those who trust me; I would be pure, for there are those who care."

But then it says, "I would be humble, for I know my weakness." Why is such a confession so difficult? It ought not to be. For human nature, whether in friend or marriage partner, will respond dramatically to the honest admission of our own weakness and our own need. Such honesty rules out pretense and sham. It rules out compulsive defending of the personality. Rather, it encourages honest prayer.

Jeanette Struchen has written some "prayers to pray without really trying." But one of them, it seems to me, might take a little courage:

> I need a wrecking crew, Lord.
> I keep building little shabby walls—
>   ego to hide my shortcomings,

When the Rain Falls

>   pride to defend my dishonesty,
>   personal desires to separate me from Your will.
> I put up foundations of prejudice and towers of
>   overconfidence.
> I pile up attitudes into blockades and fortify
>   them with slingshot opinions.
> I erect mighty convictions and brace them up
>   with sand.

I have been reading some of the prayers of the inner city kids, in their own language. Carl Burke has gathered them together.* Here is one that touches a response in any relationship where communication has broken down:

> Dear God—
> Why do religious people
> Always know they
> Are so right
> When they don't give
> Us a chance to talk?

And here is one that is simple, honest, and difficult to say:

> I'm sorry—
> But not sure what that means.
> I'm ashamed—
> But not sure of what.

---

*Carl F. Burke, *Treat Me Cool, Lord* (New York: Association Press, 1968). Used by permission.

It makes me think of the words of Paul Tournier: "There is no learned discussion about false or true guilt, but in His grace God receives all those who are ashamed." We need not analyze our guilt, or understand it. But we can feel it, and deeply mean it.

And here is one more prayer from the city streets. Underneath its language you will see a picture of human behavior that is uncannily accurate:

> Lord, we know You s'pose to guide us with Your hand,
> But we don't let You put a finger on us,
> We know You s'pose to guide us with Your eye,
> But we stay outta Your sight;
> That You s'pose to be with us all the time,
> But we make believe You ain't here;
> That You can teach us right from wrong,
> But we ain't listenin' to You,
> Even though You know best.

Sound familiar? Who of us has been so frank to acknowledge our own maneuverings? Does this prayer from the inner city echo your own experience? Does it touch a sensitive response? I confess it does in me.

Coming still closer home is the experience of Rosalind Rinker. She relates how she, with two other young missionaries in China, determined in their prayer group to make their prayers personal and conversational and honest. One day she decided that her prayer would be one of admission concerning her strong tendency to be "bossy"—to imagine her ideas superior to those of others and far more workable.

"Lord," she began, "if I have been . . ." She stopped,

When the Rain Falls

sensing she was giving herself a "leg to stand on," which she really didn't mean to do. She started over. "Dear Lord, I sometimes have a tendency to . . ." She stopped again. She knew that at that moment she was still not taking any personal responsibility for her actions and attitude. She started a third time—with determination. "Dear Lord Jesus, forgive me for always thinking my way is better, and for always wanting to 'boss' everything—" She stopped, knowing she had finally revealed the truth without rationalizing.

Her friends picked up this fragment of conversational prayer. One of them said, "Thank You, Lord, for Ros's honesty." And the other prayed, "Yes, thank You. We have always known she was like this, but it sure helps us to hear her admit it."

When I first heard this story, I knew she was talking about me. For I must confess that I am sure there have been times when my family would have been deeply relieved to hear me pray in a spirit like that, acknowledging that I, too, make mistakes and sometimes make others unhappy. Who of us cannot think of times when the way would have been much happier for the family if there had been more of this kind of honesty?

Why is it that we love each other more when mistakes and weaknesses are admitted? In fact, is a home ever likely to disintegrate while two marriage partners join hands before an understanding God and face their problems honestly? Hardly!

There will be stress. There will be rain. And there may have been disloyalty. But God has not been caught unprepared. Long before science taught us that we had a subconscious mind to contend with, with inherited tendencies to selfishness, with filth that rises to rest like scum upon the surface of the mind—I say, before we ever learned these terms, the Word of God showed us how even these deepest areas could be cleansed and changed.

Thank God, we don't need to accept ourselves as we are. Conversion is possible even for the subconscious mind. When a man consents to the healing stroke of Omnipotence, when a man invites the divine invasion of his soul, he can know that that touch of purity will sink to the depths and cleanse and sweeten and purify. It will leave him clean. And it will leave him kind!

What would you give for a cleansing like that? What would such a change do for your home? What would such a possibility mean to those you love? You've promised them the best. Heaven will help you give it!

It is our hope that the content of this volume has stimulated your thinking and that your friendship with Jesus has taken on new meaning.

Books by George Vandeman

Happiness Wall to Wall
Destination Life
Hammers in the Fire
A Day to Remember
Planet in Rebellion
Papa, Are You Going to Die?
Is Anybody Driving?
Sail Your Own Seas
The Day the Cat Jumped
How to Live With a Tiger
How to Burn Your Candle
The Impersonation Game
Tying Down the Sun
The Stuff of Survival
Showdown in the Middle East

Pacific Press Publishing Association

Happiness Wall to Wall

photography/dale rusch